MINNESOTA AACR 2 TRAINERS SERIES

Edward Swanson, Series Editor

Number 1. *Cataloging Motion Pictures and Videorecordings*, by Nancy B. Olson. 1991

Cataloging Motion Pictures and Videorecordings

By Nancy B. Olson

Edited by Edward Swanson

Soldier Creek Press
Lake Crystal, Minnesota
1991

First Edition
Second printing (minor corrections) June 1992

Olson, Nancy B.
        Cataloging motion pictures and videorecordings / by Nancy B. Olson ; edited by
Edward Swanson. -- 1st ed. -- Lake Crystal, Minn. : Soldier Creek Press, 1991.
        ix, 150 p. : ill. ; 28 cm. -- (Minnesota AACR 2 trainers series ; no. 1)

        Includes indexes.
        ISBN: 0-936996-38-2

        1. Cataloging of motion pictures -- Handbooks, manuals, etc. 2. Cataloging of video
recordings -- Handbooks, manuals, etc. I. Swanson, Edward, 1941- II. Series.

Z695.64.O67 1991
025.3473

Cover art by David Kaun

Soldier Creek Press
P. O. Box 734
Lake Crystal, Minnesota 56055-0734 USA

Nancy B. Olson, President
Edward Swanson, Editor-in-Chief
Sharon Olson, Managing Editor

This book was created electronically using Micorsoft Word and Aldus PageMaker on the Apple Macintosh IIfx
computer. Printing and binding by Corporate Graphics International.

TABLE OF CONTENTS

FOREWORD

This manual, the first in the new series of manuals of the Minnesota AACR 2 Trainers to use the 1988 revision of the *Anglo-American Cataloguing Rules*, second edition, is based on *A Manual of AACR 2 Examples for Motion Pictures and Videorecordings* by Nancy B. Olson and Jean Aichele (Soldier Creek Press, 1981). The 1981 manual had 21 complete examples and 8 to be completed by the user, most of which were educational 16 mm films. This manual has 40 examples, complete with subject headings, classification numbers, and MARC coding and tagging.

The Minnesota AACR 2 Trainers

One of the problems of implementation of AACR 2 was the need to teach new cataloging rules to all catalogers in the country. The process used in Minnesota is detailed in the following article by Edward Swanson, as reprinted from the *Minitex Messenger* (vol. 6, no. 2, Sept. 1980).

AACR 2 in Minnesota
by Edward Swanson

Planning for AACR 2 in Minnesota began in the winter of 1979 when invitations to nominate persons to attend the Introductory Program on the Anglo-American Cataloguing Rules, Second Edition, Preconference in Dallas in June 1979 were mailed to library associations, state library agencies, and other groups throughout the United States. Those selected to attend the Preconference were to be trained in AACR 2 and then would form the core group of trainers in their home states. The Preconference was planned by the Ad Hoc AACR 2 Introductory Program Committee, established by the ALA Resources and Technical Services Division and chaired by Doralyn Hickey.

Thirteen Minnesotans, nominated by MLA, MEMO, MINITEX, OPLIC, SMILE, CLIC, Mankato State University, the University of Minnesota Libraries, and the University of Minnesota Library School, were selected to attend from Minnesota. They included:

Jean Aichele, St. Cloud State University;
Julia Blixrud, MINITEX;
Helen Gbala, College of St. Catherine;
Mary Hanley, University of Minnesota Bio-Medical Library;
Helen Liu, University of Minnesota;
Sue Mahmoodi, OPLIC;
Phyllis Marion, University of Minnesota Law Library;
Barbara N. Moore, Mankato State University;
Tom Nicol, St. John's University;
Nancy Olson, Mankato State University;
Irene Schilling, Augsburg College;
Wesley Simonton, University of Minnesota Library School;
Jan Snesrud, University of Minnesota.

Marilyn H. Jones, University of Minnesota, and Edward Swanson, Minnesota Historical Society, who were members of the Introductory Program Committee, served as trainers at the Preconference.

The Preconference began with four videotapes dealing with the history of code revison, description, choice of access points, and form of headings. Small group sessions dealt in depth with description, choice, and form. The final programs at the Preconference dealt with workshop planning and effective communication in a small group setting.

The 15 Minnesotans, soon to become known as the Minnesota AACR 2 Trainers, began meeting in July to plan the training sessions in Minnesota.

The first program was held in October at the U of M St. Paul Campus. "Planning for AACR 2" began with a description of the major changes in AACR 2, given by Wesley Simonton. Nancy Olson discussed the Library of Congress's decision about adopting the code, Tom Nicol related decisions made by OCLC, and Phyllis Marion presented options a library can adopt in relating entries in its catalogs created under AACR 2 and under earlier codes. A panel composed of Walt Dunlap, Arrowhead Library System; Sanford Berman, Hennepin County Library; Barbara N. Moore; and Helen Liu described options for various types and sizes of libraries in coping with the changes.

At the November 1979 meeting of the Minnesota Library Association, Frances Hinton, head of the processing department at the Free Library of Philadelphia, spoke on changes to forms of headings that will occur after the adoption of AACR 2. Hinton was a member of the ALA Catalog Code Revision Committee and deputy ALA representative to the Joint Steering Committee. She is now the ALA representative to the reconstituted Joint Steering Committee and its chair.

The Trainers spent the winter months preparing for the first series of workshops, held in April and May at six locations around the state. These workshops dealt with changes in descriptions, choice of entry, and form of headings under AACR 2. The Trainers divided into three groups, each group covering one of these topics. In addition to planning the sessions to be given on the particular topic, each group also assembled cataloging examples and copy that were compiled into a publication, *A Manual of AACR 2 Examples*. This manual was distributed to each workshop attendee as the basic text for the workshop sessions. In addition, it has been made available for sale and some 1500 copies have been sold thus far throughout the United States and Canada and to librairies in such places as Iceland, Singapore, and Malaysia. The manual has received favorable reviews from various sources and has been adopted as a textbook in several library education programs.

The first workshop was held April 11, 1980, at the Hennepin County Southdale Library followed by ones at Bethany College, Winona State University, St. John's University, Bemidji State University, and the University of Minnesota, Duluth. Almost 200 librarians from all types of libraries in Minnesota attended these sessions. At each one the three major topics were covered, each taught by one or more members of the group that had worked on that topic. The workshops' reception was probably best exemplified by the remark made by a librarian who had quite a few years of cataloging experience, "I'm not afraid of it any more."

The Technical Services Section of the Minnesota Library Association sponsored a talk by Elizabeth L. Tate at its spring meeting in St. Cloud on the strategies for searching library catalogs using AACR 2 as compared with earlier cataloging codes. Formerly head of the descriptive cataloging division at the Library of Congress, Tate is the editor of *Library Resources & Technical Services*. Also at that meeting, the Minnesota Library Association honored the Minnesota AACR 2 Trainers by presenting them certificates of merit "in recognition of your contribution to the profession by giving your time, energy, and enthusiasm in promoting and teaching AACR 2 to librarians throughout Minnesota."

During the summer of 1980 the Trainers continued their work preparing for a series of workshops on cataloging of specialized types of materials. These workshops, to be held at the Sheraton Inn-Northwest in Minneapolis, Oct. 23-25, will include sessions on cataloging graphics and non-music sound recordings, serials, manuscripts, legal materials, liturgical works and sacred scriptures, early printed books, motion pictures and videorecordings, music scores and music sound recordings, cartographic materials, and three-dimensional artefacts and realia. A repeat of the spring workshops will also be offered, as well as a workshop on cataloging using the Level 1 form of description. Several of these sessions will be repeated during the three days to enable attendees to cover several topics in a short period of time.

On Thursday evening, Oct. 23, there will be a session designed for public services librarians that will cover the basic changes in AACR 2 from earlier cataloging codes. Announcements of the workshops have been mailed to libraries throughout Minnesota, as well as to members of the various library associations in the state.

Minneapolis was the site in August of one of a series of workshops on AACR 2 presented by the Library of Congress. These "LC roadshows" are being held throughout the United States, sponsored by the ALA Resources and Technical Services Division. Six senior members of the cataloging divisions at LC are at each roadshow to describe how the Library of Congress is going to apply AACR

2. Over 200 librarians from the Upper Midwest and Canada attended the Minneapolis session.

Minnesota will be well prepared for Jan. 1, 1981, the "Day-1" for AACR 2. Unlike 1967, when the first edition was adopted (or rather partially adopted) with almost no introdution, a concerted effort has been made to acquaint librairans in the state with the changes that will begin appearing in their catalogs in 1981. This would not have been possible without the Minnesota AACR 2 Trainers. These 15 people took their charge seriously and returned from the Introductory Program Preconference in Dallas ready and willing to work together to carry it out. Interestingly, this work has been carried out without any outside sponsorship or financial support. The group has worked well together, although at times the discussions over what a particular rule means did become somewhat protracted and not a little heated. The key is that the group has been able to work as a group dedicated to a single goal. And best of all, we've had fun doing it!

The October 1980 workshops mentioned in the article above were extremely successful with 200 librarians from five states registered. These workshops were repeated in October 1985 with over 100 attendees. Some of the Trainers were invited to present workshops in other states during this time.

The Trainers organized themselves to present these workshops because they were concerned. There is no state library in Minnesota, nor is there one library association to which all librarians belong. The Trainers could present workshops reaching school, public, academic, and special librarians all at the same time without regard to geographic or political boundaries. By cooperating and sharing their expertise they could present a range of workshops.

The original group of Trainers is listed above. Two of the group, Jean Aichele and Irene Schilling, are now deceased. Several others have retired, and some have left librarianship for other careers. Some have moved into administration.

The Trainers received no funds from any agency, nor did they receive any grant money to support their work. All Trainers volunteered their time (vacation time for most) and received neither pay nor honoraria for their participation in these workshops. Relatively small fees were charged participants in the workshops. Worldwide sales of the basic manual, *A Manual of AACR 2 Examples*, subsidized the workshops and the expenses of the Trainers.

The basic manual was published by Soldier Creek Press. All money received from sales of the first two editions, less actual expenses, was used to finance activities of the Minnesota AACR 2 Trainers.

ACKNOWLEDGEMENTS

My thanks to Rosie Mock for verifying the form of main and added entries in the OCLC authority file, and to Edward Swanson for his explanation of uniform titles, and for his careful editing. As always, thanks to my daughter-in-law, Sharon Olson, for her patient work with this manuscript and with all the Soldier Creek responsibilities.

CATALOGING MOTION PICTURES AND VIDEORECORDINGS

INTRODUCTION

This is a manual of descriptive cataloging of motion pictures and videorecordings following the *Anglo-American Cataloguing Rules*, second edition, 1988 revision (*AACR 2*). Motion pictures and videorecordings are to be cataloged following chapter 7 of *AACR 2*, as well as relevant rules from chapters 1, 21, and other chapters. The rules themselves are not included in this manual, but are referred to as needed.

The Library of Congress periodically issues rule interpretations, published in *Cataloging Service Bulletin (CSB)*. Rule interpretations related to the cataloging of motion pictures and videorecordings are included in this manual, with a citation to the most recent issue of *CSB* in which they appeared.

Examples include subject headings and classification numbers, neither of which are covered by *AACR 2*. Subject headings have been selected from *Library of Congress Subject Headings* (13th ed., 1990). Dewey classification numbers have been chosen from the 20th edition of DDC, LC classification numbers from the most recent schedules and their supplements.

Each example is shown in card format. The format shown on a catalog card, including its spacing and indentions, is a matter for local decision and is not controlled by *AACR 2*.

Each example also is shown with MARC codes and tags. The format used is that designed by OCLC, as it is the format with which I am most familiar.

TITLE AND STATEMENT OF RESPONSIBILITY AREA

Information for the title and statement of responsibility area of the description of a motion picture or videorecording is taken from the title and credits frames. If there are no title or credits frames, the information may be taken from the label on the cassette or reel, from a container, from accompanying material, from any other source, or may be supplied by the cataloger. When the title is taken from other than the title and credits frames, the source of the title is given in a note.

The source of the title proper becomes the chief source of information for this area. Nothing taken from the chief source is bracketed. A title proper will be bracketed only when it is supplied by the cataloger. Other parts of the catalog record are bracketed only when the information contained in a particular area is taken from a source other than the chief source for that area.

Title proper (7.1B)

One of the problems in cataloging motion pictures and videorecordings is the wording of the title proper. The following Library of Congress rule interpretation explains the problem and gives direction.

> LCRI 7.1B1 (*CSB* 13) When credits for performer, author, director, producer, "presenter," etc., precede or follow the title in the chief source, in general do not consider them as part of the title proper, even though the language used integrates the credits with the title. (In the examples below the italicized words are to be considered the title proper.)
>> Twentieth Century Fox presents *Star wars*
>> Steve McQueen in *Bullitt*
>> Ed Asner as *Lou Grant*
>> Jerry Wald's production of *The Story on page one*
>> *Ordinary people* starring Mary Tyler Moore and Donald Sutherland
>> *Thief*, with James Caan
> This does not apply to the following cases:
>> 1) the credit is within the title, rather than preceding or following it;
>>> CBS special report
>>> IBM—close up
>>> IBM puppet shows

2) the credit is actually a fanciful statement aping a credit;
       Little Roquefort in Good mousekeeping
3) the credit is represented by a possessive immediately preceding the remainder of the title.
       Neil Simon's Seems like old times

Title proper examples from this manual:

```
Who framed Roger Rabbit?
Frank Capra's It's a wonderful life
Star wars. Episode IV, A new hope
[Butterfield reunion]
```

General material designation (7.1C)

The two general material designations permitted by rule 1.1C1 for this material are "motion picture" and "videorecording".

Parallel titles (7.1D)

Parallel titles are recorded following a space-equals sign-space.

    Example: `In praise of hands [GMD] = Hommage aux mains`

Other title information (7.1E)

Other title information found in the title and credits frames is recorded following the general material designation, preceded by a space-colon-space. If similar information is found elsewhere on the item, it is recorded in a note if considered important.

    Examples: `The making of a legend [GMD] : Gone with the wind`
                 `Star trek [GMD] : the motion picture`
                 `Spellbound [GMD] : the razor sequence`

Statements of responsibility (7.1F)

Films generally have extensive credits. Names of persons and of corporate bodies having major importance in the production of a film are to be named in the statement of responsibility. Other names, if and as needed, are to be recorded in notes.

When information is used in the statement of responsibility from the title and credits frames, it is transcribed exactly as found. If used in a formal note, it is edited and used according to the rules for formal notes.

An LCRI explains the Library of Congress policy on statement of responsibility information. (See also the LCRI for 7.7B6.)

> LCRI 7.1F1 (*CSB* 36) When deciding whether to give names in the statement of responsibility or in a note, generally give the names in the statement of responsibility when the person or body has some degree of overall responsibility; use the note area for others who are responsible for only one segment or one aspect of the work. Be liberal about making exceptions to the general policy when the person's or body's responsibility is important in relation to the content of the work, i.e., give such important people and bodies in the statement of responsibility even though they may have only partial responsibility. For example, the name of a rock music performer who is the star of a performance on a videorecording may be given in the statement of responsibility even if his/her responsibility is limited to the performance.

Ain't that America / John Cougar Mellencamp
Normally the Library of Congress considers producers, directors, and writers ... as having some degree of overall responsibility and gives them in the statement of responsibility.

Examples: Who framed Roger Rabbit? [videorecording] / Touchstone Pictures and Amblin Entertainment in association with Silver Screen Partners III ; directed by Robert Zemeckis ; produced by Robert Watts & Frank Marshall ; screenplay by Jeffrey Price & Peter S. Seaman ; executive producers, Steven Spielberg & Kathleen Kennedy ; director of animation, Richard Williams
     Irving Berlin's Holiday Inn [videorecording] / a Paramount picture ; produced and directed by Mark Sandrich ; screen play by Claude Binyon ; adaptation by Elmer Rice ; lyrics and music by Irving Berlin
     The Trouble with tribbles [videorecording] / produced by Gene L. Coon ; directed by Joseph Pevney ; written by David Gerrold

EDITION AREA

Edition information is transcribed in this area, using any abbreviations permitted in *AACR 2* Appendix B for the area. Edition information taken from the container must be bracketed.

Examples: Major rev.
50th anniversary limited ed.
Color version
Letterbox format

PUBLICATION, DISTRIBUTION, ETC., AREA

The prescribed sources of information for area 4 include the chief source of information (the title and credits screens) and any accompanying material. Accompanying material includes a teacher's guide, but does not include the container of a videocassette. Therefore, any information taken from the container of a videocassette must be bracketed.

Place of publication, distribution, etc. (7.4C)

The place of publication is given first in this area. This place of publication or distribution for videocassettes is given only on the container in most cases. If so, it must be bracketed.

Examples: Livonia, Mich.
        Standard abbreviations for state names are found in Appendix B of *AACR 2*.
Universal City, CA
        Postal abbreviations for state names may only be used when found on the item.
N[ew] Y[ork]
        Missing information is to be supplied
[United States]
        If one does not know the city or state, supply the name of the country. Appendix B of *AACR 2* does not permit the abbreviation U.S. in this area.

Name of publisher, distributor, etc. (7.4D)

The name of the publisher or distributor is given here, in the form found on the item. We may choose to shorten the name, but, according to LCRI 1.4D2 (*CSB* 47) we no longer are to attempt to judge how well the name is known internationally. The name of the publisher or distributor usually appears on the first of the title/credits frames of the motion picture or video.

> Examples: MCA Videocassette
>   CBS/Fox Video
>   Warner Home Video

Date of publication, distribution, etc. (7.4F)

The date of publication, distribution, or release is to be given here. A film might have several dates of importance, including the year it was made originally, the year it was released as a video, the year it had color added, the year the physical form in hand was copyrighted. The date to be used in this area is the publication/distribution date of the item in hand. Other dates may be included in notes.

The latest date found on the item is used in area 4, as it is assumed the latest date is the date of publication. An assumed date is to be bracketed.

If the date of publication of the item in hand is taken from the container, it must be bracketed. The film may show only the original date of production. The container may list a copyright date that is more recent. The copyright date is used as the basis for an assumed date of publication of the item.

The date on the container may be contained in some phrase indicating it is the date of copyright of the container artwork and/or text. It may still be used as the basis for an assumed date of publication of the item in hand. It would be bracketed as an assumed date, or bracketed as coming from the container; it would only be given without brackets if found on the film itself or on a guide or printed material accompanying the item.

Copyright renewal dates may be ignored.

> Examples: c1987
>   [198-]
>   1989

PHYSICAL DESCRIPTION AREA

The physical description area includes four parts: extent of item, other physical details, dimensions, and accompanying material.

Extent of item (7.5B)

The number of physical items, and the name of these items, are given here. Trade names or specifications related to the equipment needed no longer are included here, but are given in a note.

Playing time is added, in parentheses. This playing time is given exactly as stated on the item.

Special rules are provided for videodiscs. If the videodisc is a film, playing time is given in the normal manner. If the videodisc consists of still images, playing time may be given if appropriate, or the number of frames/images may be given. If the videodisc contains both moving images and still images, the contents are better explained in a note.

Other physical details (7.5C)

For most collections, the information recorded here will be an indication of color and of sound. For archival collections, aspect ratio, special projection characteristics, and projection speed may be given. Stereo sound is recorded in area 4 as "sd." and a note is used to specify the stereo aspect.

Dimensions (7.5D)

The width of motion picture film is given in millimeters, that of videotape in inches. The videodisc diameter is given in inches.

Accompanying material (7.5E)

Accompanying material is counted and named as appropriate, with the physical description expanded as necessary. Any further description of the accompanying material may be given in a note.

Container

Information about the container and its size may be given at the end of the physical description area. If the items in the container include those listed in the accompanying material part of area 5, the "in container" phrase follows the accompanying material statement. If there is no accompanying material statement, or if the container does not include those items listed in the accompanying material statement, the "in container" phrase follows the dimensions.

```
Examples:  1 videodisc (119 min.) : sd., col. and b&w ; 12 in. + 1 booklet
     (32 p. : ill. ; 22 cm.)
        1 videocassette (53 min.) : sd., col. with b&w sequences ;
     1/2 in.
        2 videocassettes (ca. 3 hrs., 59 min.) : sd., col. ; 1/2 in.
     + 1 booklet ([5] p. : col. ill. ; 22 cm.) in container 23 x 27
     x 4 cm.
        1 film reel (5 min.) : sd., col. ; 16 mm.
```

SERIES AREA

Series statements are recorded in this area. If the series information is taken from the container it must be bracketed.

```
Examples:  Walt Disney classics
           Christmas classics series
```

NOTE AREA

Two or more notes, or types of notes, may be combined into one.

```
Examples:  An animated adaptation of the book of the same title by J.R.R.
           Tolkien.
           Documentary about making the movie Gone with the wind.
```

Quoted notes are used when one wants to use information exactly as found in the credits, on the label or container, or elsewhere. The source of the information must be cited if it is other than the chief source of information.

```
           "The official World Series video"--Container.
           "An OCLC video communications program."
```

Formal notes begin with an introductory word or phrase followed by a colon. Formal notes follow a defined structure and use defined punctuation.

```
     Cast: Clark Gable, Vivien Leigh, Leslie Howard, Olivia De
Havilland.
     Credits: Music, Alan Silvestri ; special visual effects,
Industrial Light & Magic
```

Informal notes do not follow any defined pattern

```
     Booklet describes and illustrates the film production
```

Notes are given in the order of the rules in *AACR 2*. However, any note may be moved into the first position if it is considered the most important.

Nature or form note (7.7B1)

A note is used to name or explain the nature or form of a motion picture or videorecording, unless the information is obvious from the rest of the description or is combined with other information in a summary or other note.

```
Examples:  Documentary
           Opera
           "An OCLC video communications program"
```

Language note (7.7B2)

The language of the spoken, sung, or written content of the item is named unless it is apparent from the rest of the description.

```
Example:  Dubbed into English
```

LCRI 7.4F2 (*CSB* 33) If the videorecording incorporates closed-captioning for the hearing impaired, make the following note:
Closed-captioned for the hearing impaired.

The presence of closed-captioning may be indicated by words and/or symbols on the package. There may also be some indication in the credits. The symbol looks like a television screen with a tail. It may appear on a container with no indication of its meaning.

Note for source of title proper (7.7B3)

If the title proper is taken from other than the title and credits screen, name the source of title in this note.

```
Examples:  Title from container
           Title supplied by cataloger
```

Note on variations in title (7.7B4)

Other forms of the title may appear on the item. Significant variations are given in notes. Remember, information must appear somewhere in the bibliographic record before added entries for that information may be made.

Examples: Title on container: Batman, the movie
             Title on cassette: Walt Disney's Cinderella. Title on
             container: Walt Disney's classic Cinderella

Note on parallel titles and other title information (7.7B5)

Parallel titles, titles in other languages, and other title information not recorded in area 1 are noted here if considered important.

Example: Title on container: La cage aux folles = Birds of a
            feather

Statements of responsibility notes (7.7B6)

There are two statements of responsibility notes, one for cast and one for credits.

Cast

Featured players, performers, narrators, and/or presenters may be listed in a cast note, or these names may be incorporated into the contents note. The role played by a cast member may be added after the name of the performer in parentheses.

Examples: Cast: Cary Grant, Katharine Hepburn, James Stewart, Ruth
             Hussey
             Voices: Orson Bean, Richard Boone, Hans Conried, John
             Huston, Otto Preminger, Cyril Ritchard, Theodore
             Cast: Judith Blegen (Gretel), Frederica von Stade
             (Hansel), Jean Kraft (Gertrude), Michael Devlin (Peter),
             Diane Kesling (Sandman), Betsy Norden (Dewfairy) ;
             Metropolitan Opera Orchestra, Metropolitan Opera Chorus,
             Thomas Fulton, conductor

Credits

Others who have contributed to the artistic and/or technical production, but who are not named in the statement of responsibility, may be named here. The following LCRI provides guidance, but keep in mind the needs of your own patrons as you make these notes. You may want to use more credits, or you may want to use fewer credits.

> LCRI 7.7B6 (*CSB* 22) For audiovisual items, generally list persons (other than producers, directors, and writers) or corporate bodies who have contributed to the artistic and technical production of a work in a credits note.
> Give the following persons or bodies in the order in which they are listed below. Preface each name or group of names with the appropriate term(s) of function.
> photographer(s); camera; cameraman/men; cinematographer
> animator(s)
> artist(s); illustrator(s); graphics
> film editor(s); photo editor(s); editor(s)
> narrator(s); voice(s)
> music
> consultant(s); adviser(s)
> Do not include the following persons or bodies performing these functions:
> assistants or associates
> production supervisors or coordinators

project or executive editors
technical advisers or consultants
audio or sound engineers
writers of discussion, program, or teacher's guides
other persons making only a minor or purely technical contribution

A cataloging decision made at the Library of Congress, published in the *Music Cataloging Bulletin* (vol. 20, no. 6) instructs us to use the same punctuation in performer notes as would be used in the statement of responsibility. The semicolon is set off by a space on each side. This punctuation is followed throughout the other chapters for credits notes.

Examples: `Credits: Music, Alan Silvestri ; special visual effects,`
         `Industrial Light & Magic`
              `"Musical score written and directed by Dimitri Tiomkin"`

Edition and history note (7.7B7)

Information relating to the edition being described or to the history of the item is given in this note.

LCRI 7.7B7 (*CSB* 15) When an item is known to have an original master in a different medium and the production or release date of the master is more than two years earlier than that of the item being cataloged, give an edition/history note.
Originally produced as motion picture in [year]
Originally issued as filmstrip in [year]
Make a similar note when an item is known to have been previously produced or issued (more than two years earlier) if in a different medium, but the original medium is unknown.
Previously produced as motion picture in [year]
Previously issued as slide set in [year]
If the date of production or release of an original master or an earlier medium is unknown or if the difference between its production or release date and the production or release date of the item being cataloged is two years or less, indicate the availability of the other medium or media in a note according to 7.7B16 and 8.7B16.
Produced also as slide set.
Issued also as slide set and videorecording.
Note: The use of production versus release dates is left to the cataloger's judgment. Make the note that seems best to give information about either production or release of other formats on a case-by-case basis.

Examples: `Originally produced as motion picture in 1946`
         `Based on the book: Who censored Roger Rabbit? / by Gary`
         `K. Wolf`
         `Originally produced as motion picture in 1956; remake of`
         `1940 film, The Philadelphia story`
         `Recorded at a performance of the Metropolitan Opera, Dec.`
         `26, 1982`

Note on publication, distribution, etc., and date (7.7B8)

Notes may be made on any publication or distribution details considered important but not included in area 4 of the bibliographic description. The date of the original production may also be included when different from the date of publication, distribution, etc. Country of original release may be included if not stated or implied elsewhere in the description.

Example: A co-production of Les Productions artistes associés and
Da ma produzione SPA, originally produced as French-Italian
motion picture in 1979. Released in the United States by
United Artists

LCRI 7.7B9 (*CSB* 13) When a foreign firm, etc., is given in the source as emanator or originator, do not assume that the item was either made or released in that country if not so stated. Instead use the note
A foreign film (Yugoslavia)
For a U.S. emanator and a foreign producer or a foreign emanator and a U.S. producer, do not make the note.
… / Learning Corporation of America ; [produced by] Earl Rosen and Associates
(Earl Rosen and Associates is a Canadian firm)

Physical description notes (7.7B10)

Many kinds of information may be recorded in this note, including sound characteristics, length of film or tape, color, form of print, film base, videorecording system, generation of copy, special projection requirements, and duration and number of frames for videodiscs. Much of this information is of interest only to archival film collections. For most libraries the types of information recorded here will concentrate on sound characteristics and the videorecording system needed for playback.

Because the information on a container is not presented in any standardized format, it might be best simply to copy all of that information into a quoted note.

If desired, this note can be moved into position as the first note.

Sound characteristics

Examples: Stereo
"Digitally processed; Dolby surround stereo; hi-fi"--
Container
"Videophonic sound, digitally enhanced for stereo; Dolby
system"--Container
"Digital audio, Dolby surround"--Container
"Presented in digitally mastered hi-fi stereo"--Container

Videorecording system

Examples: VHS
VHS hi-fi
"LaserVision; extended play; digital sound; chapter
search"--Container

Note on accompanying material (7.7B11)

Details about the accompanying material may be given in this note.

Examples: Booklet describes and illustrates the film production
Booklet includes program notes and synopsis

Series note (7.7B12)

Note may be made of any series information not already given.

Example: Previously issued in series: Walt Disney classics

Dissertation note (7.7B13)

If the item is a dissertation, the standard dissertation note is made.

> Example: Thesis (M.S.)--St. Cloud State University, 1977

Audience note (7.7B14)

The intended audience, intellectual level, or the Motion Picture Association of America (MPAA) rating of a film may be given in this note if the information is stated on the item, container, or accompanying material.

> Examples: Rated PG
> Intended audience: Grades 6-9
> "Suitable for all ages"--Container

Note on other formats (7.7B16)

Other formats in which the item has been distributed may be listed here.

> Example: Issued also as laserdisc

Summary (7.7B17)

Provide a brief objective summary unless the content is obvious from the title and other description. Information from one or more of the notes listed above may be combined with contents information in this summary. The note may be based on information from the container, it may be quoted from the container, or it may be excerpted from the container or from other sources. Summary writing is a challenge, but it can be fun.

> Examples: Summary: An animated adaptation of the book by J.R.R. Tolkien. Concerns the adventures of Bilbo Baggins, the Hobbit, and 13 dwarfs as they attempt to recapture their treasure from Smaug, the terrible dragon
> Summary: "The Enterprise receives a top priority order to protect Space Station K-7 ... Involved in a running quarrel with both the Federation Undersecretary for Agriculture and the Klingon Commander, Captain Kirk fails to notice the sudden popularity of a new fad—Tribbles"--Container
> Summary: Princess Leia is captured and held hostage by the evil Imperial forces in their effort to take over the galactic Empire

Contents (7.7B18)

A contents note lists the titles of the individual works, or parts, contained in the physical item being cataloged. The contents note includes statements of responsibility not already included in area 1 and the duration of each item if known. A brief description of each title or part may be added in brackets, combining summary information within the contents.

Informal notes may be made on partial contents.

> Examples: Contents: For whom the bulls toil (1953) -- Lion down (1950) -- A knight for a day (1945)
> Preceded by Pepsi commercial: I'm bad

LCRI 1.7B18 (*CSB* 49) In a formal contents note, do not capitalize the first recorded volume designation (unless called for by the rules of the language involved). Also, for "volume" and "volumes", use "v."

> Contents: pt. 1. The cause of liberty (24 min.) -- pt. 2. The impossible war (25 min.)
> *not* Contents: Pt. 1 The cause of liberty (24 min) ...

Notes on numbers (7.7B19)

Numbers other than ISBNs or ISSN may be recorded here if considered to be important.

Example: `On label: OCLC #41699280 [i.e., 14699280]`

Notes on copy being described, library's holdings, and restrictions on use (7.7B20)

Note may be made concerning the copy being described, the holdings of the cataloging library, and any restrictions on the use of the copy held by that library. Restrictions applying to all copies of an item belong in the "audience" note.

Example: `Use restricted to law enforcement students`

"With" notes (7.7B21)

When two or more separately titled items are packaged together without a collective title, they may be cataloged using "with" notes. A separate bibliographic record is made for each. The note on each bibliographic record gives the title proper of the other bibliographic records prepared for the package.

Example: `With: Multidimensional data analysis`

ACCESS POINTS

After the descriptive cataloging is completed, main and added entries are chosen following the rules given in chapter 21 of *AACR 2*.

Main entry

Motion pictures and videorecordings may be entered under personal author, corporate author, title, or uniform title. Very few commercial films would fall under the rule for entry under personal author, as most films have numerous persons and corporate bodies sharing the creative responsibilities.

Entry under corporate body is quite restrictive. A film issued by a corporate body and about the corporate body might be entered under the heading for that corporate body, if it fits into one of the categories in rule 21.1B2. Few other items would be likely to receive corporate main entry, with the exception of some music videos. See rule 21.1B2 for a list of categories for which corporate body main entry is permitted.

Most motion pictures and videorecordings are entered under title proper.

Uniform title

Some motion pictures and/or videorecordings might need a uniform title main entry when "the title of the work is obscured by the wording of the title proper" or when there are two or more works with the same title.

LCRI 25.5B (*CSB* 46) Conflict resolution

Radio and Television Programs

Add the qualifier "(Radio program)" or "(Television program)" to the title of a radio or television program whenever the program is needed in a secondary entry and the title is the same as a Library of Congress subject heading or the title has been used as the title of another work. (It does not matter if the other work is entered under title or under a name heading.) This same uniform title for the radio or television program must be used in all entries for the particular work. (Existing records in which the radio or television program has been used as a main or added entry must be adjusted.)

Motion Pictures

If a motion picture is entered under a title proper that is the same as the title proper of another motion picture (or other work), do not assign a uniform title to either to distinguish them, even if there are multiple editions of either work. However, if a motion picture is needed in a secondary entry and the title of the motion picture is the same as a Library of Congress subject heading or the title is the same as the title of another work, add the qualifier "(Motion picture)" to the title of the motion picture. This same uniform title must be used in all entries for the particular work. Existing records in which the motion picture is used as a main or secondary entry must be adjusted.

These are *qualifiers* added in parentheses, *not* GMDs. Use of uniform title main entry is illustrated by several examples in this manual.

Added entries

LCRI 21.29 (*CSB* 12) Order of added entries.
　　Give added entries in the following order:
　　　　1. Personal name;
　　　　2. Personal name/title;
　　　　3. Corporate name;
　　　　4. Corporate name/title;
　　　　5. Uniform title (all instances of works entered under title);
　　　　6. Title traced as Title-period;
　　　　7. Title traced as Title-colon, followed by a title;
　　　　8. Series.
　　For arrangement within any one of these groupings, generally follow the order in which the justifying data appear in the bibliographic description. If such a criterion is not applicable, use judgment.

LCRI 21.29D (*CSB* 45) Added entries for audiovisual materials
　　In making added entries for audiovisual materials, follow the general rules in 21.29 and apply, in addition to those in 21.30, the following guidelines:
　　　　1. Make added entries for all openly named persons or corporate bodies who have contributed to the creation of the item, with the following exceptions:
　　　　　　a. Do not make added entries for persons (producers, directors, writers, etc.) if there is a production company, unit, etc., for which an added entry is made, unless their contributions are significant, e.g. the animator of an animated film, the producer/director of a student film, the director of a theatrical film, the film maker or developer of a graphic item attributed as author on the data sheet and/or prominently named on the accompanying material ("a film by").

In the absence of a production company, unit, etc., make added entries for those persons who are listed as producers, directors, and writers. Make additional added entries for other persons only if their contributions are significant.

b. If a person, film maker, developer of a graphic item, etc., is the main entry heading, do not make added entries for other persons who have contributed to the production, unless the production is known to be the joint responsibility or collaboration of the persons or the contributions are significant.

2. Make added entry headings for all corporate bodies named in the publication, distribution, etc., area.

3. Make added entries for all featured players, performers, and narrators with the following exceptions:

a. If, for a motion picture or videorecording, the main entry is under the heading for a performing group (in accordance with 21.1B2e), do not make added entries under the headings for persons performing as members of that group. If a person's name, however, appears in conjunction with and preceding or following the name of the group, do not consider him or her to be a member of the group.

b. If there are many players (actors, actresses, etc.), make added entries under the headings for those that are given prominence in the chief source of information. If that cannot be used as a criterion, make added entries under the headings for each if there are no more than three.

4. Similarly, make added entries under the headings for persons in a production who are interviewers or interviewees, delivering lectures, addresses, etc., or discussing their lives, ideas, work, etc., and who are not chosen as the main entry.

An extensive LCRI explains how to construct added entries for works.

LCRI 21.30M (*CSB* 45) Analytical entries

Added Entries for Works

Added entries for works reflect the type of main entry heading of the work being cataloged in the tracing as follows:

Type of main entry	*Type of added entry*
Personal or corporate name	Name heading/uniform title
Title	Uniform title
Uniform title	Title

The pharase "added entries for works" in these instructions is intended to encompass all the various types of added entries listed above.

Added entries for works are of two types: analytical and simple. They are made on the basis of various rules, some of which prescribe an analytical added entry in explicit terms, others of which do not. Whenever the added entry is made to furnish an access point to the substance of a work contained in the item being cataloged, it should be an analytical added entry (e.g., 21.7B1, 21.13B1, 21.19A1). If the added entry serves only to provide an approach to the item being cataloged through a related work, however, and the text of this work is not present in the item being cataloged, then a simple added entry for the work is appropriate (e.g., 21.12B1, 21.28B1, 21.30G1).

The relationship that is expressed between works by means of an added entry, either analytical or simple, is limited to a single access point, namely, that of the main entry. An added entry in the form of the main entry heading for a work provides the sole access to the work; do not trace in addition any added entries for that work's title (when main entry is under a name heading), joint author, editor, compiler, translator, etc.

Analytical Added Entries

Formulate analytical added entries as follows:

Type of analytical a.e.	*Components*
Name heading/title	Heading in catalog entry form plus uniform title
Title	Uniform title
Uniform title	Uniform title

In addition, following the uniform title, provide the language (if appropriate) and the publication date of the item being cataloged. In making analytical added entries, note expecially the following details:

1. Reduce the publication date to a simple four digit form that most nearly represents the publication date (of the first volume or part if more than one) given in the publication, distribution, etc., area. Convert a hyphen to a zero.
2. Do not abbreviate the names of languages.
3. Do not enclose uniform titles within brackets.
4. Do not give in the tracing a title found in the item being cataloged that is different from the uniform title.

Simple Added Entries

Formulate simple added entries as follows:

Type of simple added entry	*Components*
Name heading/title	Heading in catalog entry form plus uniform title
Title	Uniform title
Uniform title	Uniform title

Note that subject entries for works are formulated in the same manner as simple added entries.

Comments: Note that these guidelines call for all headings to be in uniform title form. Different forms of a title would be handled by cross-references, or through an authority system. For those of us working in less-than-ideal worlds, we need to make added entries for the titles in other forms. By definition, these are not uniform titles.

Remember the needs of your patrons as you make added entries; you may need to make more added entries, or fewer.

Form of entry

Rules for form of each type of entry are in *AACR 2* chapters 22-25. All added entries in examples in this book have been checked against the online authority file in OCLC.

SUBJECT CATALOGING

Subject cataloging, or subject analysis, includes both subject headings and classification. Neither of these processes is controlled or determined by the *Anglo-American Cataloguing Rules*. A library is free to choose whatever type of subject headings and/or classification it wants to use.

The following Library of Congress guidelines, from *Cataloging Service Bulletin* 48, are LC's own guidelines for subject headings and classification of films. They also include some MARC coding and tagging instructions.

Guidelines for Subject Cataloging of Visual Materials

For convenience, the words film and films are used throughout these guidelines to refer to any type of visual material, including motion pictures, filmstrips, video recordings, and slides.

1. *Target audience.* Films are assigned one of the following MARC codes for target audience:

a Age 0-5 (preschool through kindergarten)
b Age 6-8 (primary)
c Age 9-15 (intermediate through junior high)
d Age 16-19 (senior high)
e Adult
f Special audiences
g General

Films coded "a," "b," or "c" are treated as juvenile films. For classification purposes only, fiction films coded "d" are also treated as juvenile. The target audience of films coded "f" must be determined from the title, summary, or intended audience note (521 field). Films coded "e" or "g" are treated as adult films.

2. *Subject headings*
  a. *Topical films.* Since, for all practical purposes, it is impossible to browse a film collection, greater detail in subject cataloging treatment is required for films than is normally provided for books. In addition to the normal rules governing the assignment of subject headings, the below listed special rules are observed when assigning topical subject headings to non-fiction films:

1. A subject entry is made for all important topics mentioned in the summary statement. If a specific topic is emphasized in order to illustrate a more general concept, subject headings are assigned for both the specific and the genreal topics. Form subdivisions are assigned only to the extent that such subdivisions are applicable both to print and audiovisual media. The form subdivision —**Pictorial works** is not used.

520 field: Describes the highlights of Colombia, including the production of coffee.
  Subject entries: Colombia—Description and travel
                  Coffee—Colombia

520 field: Surveys the industries of India, with special emphasis on the steel industry
  Subject entries: India—Industries
                  Steel industry and trade—India

520 field: Documents the intellectual expansion in medieval Germany, as illustrated by the Nuremberg chronicle
Subject entries: Schedel, Hartmann, 1140-1514. Liber chronicarum
　　　　　　　　　　Germany—Intellectual life—History

2. When a topic is discussed in conjunction with a particular place, a subject entry is made, insofar as possible, under both the topic and place.

520 field: Describes the oases of the Sahara
Subject entries: Oases—Sahara
　　　　　　　　　　Sahara—Description and travel

520 field: Interviews with medical personnel and participants in a drug abuse treatment program in New York City
Subject entries: Drug abuse—New York (N.Y.)
　　　　　　　　　　New York (N.Y.)—Social conditions

3. When a film treats a particular person as illustrative of a profession or activity, a heading is assigned for both the person and the field of endeavor. Such films are not, as a general rule, treated as biographies.

520 field: A day in the life of prizefighter Muhammad Ali as he trains for a championship bout
Subject entries: Ali, Muhammad, 1942-
　　　　　　　　　　Boxing

520 field: How modern dance exponent Martha Graham functions as an artist and choreographer
Subject entries: Graham, Martha
　　　　　　　　　　Modern dance
　　　　　　　　　　Choreography

4. *Commercials.* A heading is assigned for the generic name of the product being advertised. A heading is also assigned for the particular advertising medium, if it is identified.

520 field: Television commercial for Bayer aspirin
Subject entries: Aspirin
　　　　　　　　　　Television advertising

b. *Fiction films.* The following headings are assigned, as appropriate, to individual fiction films:

1. Topical headings with the subdivision **—Drama** (or, in the case of juvenile fiction films, the subdivision **—Juvenile films**). Headings of this type are assigned to the same extent that such headings are assigned to individual dramas in book form (cf. *Subject Catalgoing Manual: Subject Headings*, H 1780, p. 2, sec. 4).
2. Form headings that express either genre (e.g., **Comedy films, Western films**) or technique (e.g., **Silent films, Experimental films**).
3. The form heading **Feature films** or **Short films**. **Feature films** is assigned to fiction films with a running time of 60 minutes or more. **Short films** is assigned to those with a running time of less than 60 minutes.
　　Note that headings (1) and/or (2) are assigned only as appropriate for the particular film being cataloged, but that heading (3) is required for *all* fiction films.

When more than one of these headings are assigned to a particular film, they are assigned in the order listed above.

c. *Films for the hearing impaired.* Either **Films for the hearing impaired** or **Video recordings for the hearing impaired** is assigned to all films produced with captions or sign language for viewing by the hearing impaired.

3. *LC classification number*

a. *Specificity of class numbers.* Films are assigned the most specific class numbers available in the LC classification schedules, including Cutter numbers for topics, places, or persons, if they are printed in the schedule. Cutter numbers are not included for places or individuals if the caption in the schedule reads, for example, "By region or country, A-Z," or "Individual, A-Z" and printed Cutters are not present. Shelflisting subarrangements are not provided. New topical class numbers are not established for films. If a number for the specific topic of the film has not been established, the next broader class number is assigned.

b. *Adult belles lettres.* To critical films about an individual literary author, the appropriate literary author number is assigned from the relevant subclass of the P schedule. Literary author numbers are also assigned to films of an author reading his or her work. If a specific Cutter number has not yet been established for the author, a class number is assigned with an incomplete Cutter, e.g., [PR6052.B].

Adult fiction films. The following guidelines are observed in classifying individual adult fiction films (i.e., those coded "e" or "g," as well as those that are coded "f" and that are determined to have an adult targeted audience):

1. All individual adult fiction films, except for comedy, experimental, and animated films, are classed in PN1997, provided that their primary purpose is entertainment. Films that are dramatizations of literary works are classed in literary author numbers only if their intention is clearly to teach about or criticize the author or the author's style or to provide opportunity for discussion, rather than simply to entertain. Certain series, such as *The Novel* or *The Short Story,* fall into this category.

2. Comedy films are classed in PN1995.9.C55; experimental films in PN1995.9.E96. These numbers are assigned to a film only when it is explicitly described as a comedy or experimental film in the 520 field.

3. Adult animated fiction films are classed in PN1997.5.

c. *Foreign language teaching films.* Films intended for use in teaching foreign languages are classed in the P schedules with the language being taught, rather than in the class for the special topic of the film. As a corollary, the heading [...] **language— Films for [...] speakers** is assigned as the first heading, and any special topics are brought out by assigning additional headings.

4. *Juvenile films.* Films are assigned a MARC code for targeted audience as described above. Films with the codes "a," "b," or "c" are treated as juvenile films. Films coded "f" are also treated as juvenile if it is clear from the title, summary, or intended audience note (521 field) that the film is juvenile in nature. For classification purposes only, fiction films coded "d" are treated as juvenile. Films coded "e" or "g" are not treated as juvenile. The guidelines below are observed when treating a film as juvenile.

a. *Subject headings.* The free-floating form subdivison —**Juvenile films** is used after all topical subject headings assigned. Children's literature catalogers assign bracketed juvenile headings as required.

b. *Classification.* Topical juvenile films are classed with the appropriate topic in classes A-Z, using the number for juvenile works if one is provided under the topic. All juvenile fiction films (i.e., those coded "a," "b," "c," or "d"), whether animated or live action, are classed in PZ5-90.

c. *Special categories of juvenile films*

1. *Folk tales.* When possible, a subject entry is made under the name of an individual hero or figure around whom a series of tales or legends have been told, e.g., **Bunyan, Paul (Legendary character)—Juvenile films.** An entry is also made for the form, even in the case of individual tales, e.g., **Tales—United States—Juvenile films** and **Folklore—United States—Juvenile films,** and for the category, i.e., **Children's films.**

2. *Juvenile reading films.* A subject entry is made to bring out the topic, if the film is topical, and to bring out the form. The heading **Reading (Primary, [Elementary, etc.])—Juvenile films** is generally used to bring out the form. The heading **Readers** or **Primers** is *not* used. Such films are classed in the numbers for readers in the subclasses of the P schedule.

520 field: A reading readiness film for primary grades on the subject of rain
Subject entries: Rain and rainfall—Juvenile films
Reading readiness—Juvenile films
Reading (Primary)—Juvenile films
050 field: [PE1127]

Examples in this manual have been assigned subject headings, including genre headings, as outlined in the above guidelines. For LC classification the breakdown at PN1995.9 has been used rather than the more general PN1997 in which films are alphabetized by title. The above policy is that used at LC for their cataloging of films from data sheets, none of which go into its collections. A general classification number serves as guidance for eventual users of LC catalog copy. In actual use, the subject/genre breakdown at PN19995.9 has worked well at the library for which I catalog. An online browse through the shelflist shows films of the same type classed together.

CATALOGING CERTAIN TYPES OF VIDEORECORDINGS

Three types of locally made videorecordings have been identified, and guidelines issued by the Library of Congress and by OCLC for their cataloging. These types, and their guidelines, are described here.

Locally produced videorecordings

Locally produced videorecordings include theses and dissertations, local historical events, class projects, university lectures, and home-filmed videos. These unpublished videorecordings may exist either as a unique copy, or in multiple copies for local or limited distribution.

Locally produced videorecordings should be cataloged as unpublished materials. Area 4 of the bibliographic record should contain only the date of the recording.

In this manual, see the example of a thesis by Gary J. Way and the Butterfield reunion home video as examples of locally produced videorecordings.

Locally reproduced videorecordings

Locally reproduced videorecordings are those video copies of motion pictures, other videos, or other audividual material, made with permission of the producer or distributor of the material being copied. These copies may be made as preservation copies or as circulating copies.

Copies made without permission may violate copyright laws.

The OCLC guidelines for cataloging locally reproduced videorecordings suggest two methods for handling these materials.

One suggestion is to treat the reproduction as a copy, adding a note for it to the bibliographic record of the original.

We may choose to create a new bibliographic record for the copy. The title and statement of responsibility area through the publication, distribution, etc., area are to be for the original, with the exception of the GMD, "videorecording". The physical description of the copy is to go in area 5. A note indicates the original format.

```
Originally issued as super 8 mm. film cartridge.
```

Another note indicates the copy was made with permission and gives the date of the reproduction.

If using OCLC, search for a record for a locally-made copy in the same format before entering a new record. If such copy is found, edit it rather than entering new copy.

Off-air recordings

An off-air videorecording is one taped directly from the television as it is being broadcast. This should only be done with permission "licensing" from the broadcaster or producer. The following is from *Cataloging Service Bulletin* 19.

> It has been agreed that the physical description area of a videorecording taped from a broadcast should reflect the actual copy in hand without attempting to reproduce a description of the "original" item. Many of these programs exist as published videorecordings, and existing records for the published versions could be used by libraries that own an off-the-air copy. Locally-reproduced videorecordings (e.g., preservation copies of deteriorating motion pictures, made with permission) could in most instances be treated as copies of the motion pictures. If a record for the original motion picture exists in the catalog, libraries could use the existing record and indicate the information about the copy in the notes area. If a new record were created, it should reflect the description of the original in the transcription of title and credits information, but the physical description should reflect the copy in hand ...
>
> The second major point of discussion was handling the publication, distribution, etc., area for off-the-air recordings. Some catalogers attempted to equate broadcasting with publication and use area 4 to record details of broadcasting. Since broadcasting is not publication either from a legal standpoint or in cataloging theory, this approach could not be supported. Institutions that own off-the-air copies could use existing records for published videorecordings, or if these records do not exist, catalog their copies as unpublished and not attempt to supply a name as the publisher or distributor.

The publication, distribution, etc., area for these items would contain only the date of recording. In this manual, see the example *Death and dying* as an example of an off-air videorecording.

MARC CODING AND TAGGING

The MARC coding and tagging in these examples is based on the OCLC format document, *Audiovisual Media Format*, second edition (OCLC, 1986). I will not attempt to explain all the codes, tags, indicators, etc., here, as they are all carefully explained and illustrated in that OCLC document. End-of-field marks have been omitted. The OCLC formats shown are as displayed in OCLC's PRISM service.

Fixed fields

"Ctry"

"Ctry" is coded for the country of *production* of the motion picture or videorecording, not for the country of distribution or release. This means the coding is not taken from the 260 field unless the distributor was also the producer. We know most old movies were produced in California. We may know the country in which foreign films were produced, and we put that information in the notes. It is that information that is to be coded. If the exact place is unknown, but we know the film was produced in the United States, code "xxu".

"Dat tp"

"Dates" and "Dat tp" are confusing. The discussion of "Dat tp" "r" in the *Audiovisual Media Format*, (2nd ed., OCLC, 1989, MED FF:7-10, Rev. 8911) includes a long discussion of changes that would involve reissue or re-release, and changes that would indicate the work should be treated as a new work. Point 7 of that discussion clearly indicates that "a motion picture re-released as a videorecording" is to be treated as a new work. It is not coded "r".

In the Question-and-Answer column of the Online Audiovisual Catalogers *Newsletter* (v. 4, no. 2, June 1984) Urbanski discusses coding of "Dat tp." She concludes:

Appropriate codes for commercially produced video copies of previously released motion pictures will be:
"s" if only one date is known;
"p" if release date of video and production date of the original motion picture or current video are known and there is a diffrence of at least one year between those dates;
"c" if current release and current or original copyright are known; and
"q" if a digit is missing from the date.

The USMARC format (USMARC Bibliographic, 008/06 p. 5, January 1988) gives the following information: "For moving images, if a work with identical content but in a different medium has a later release date than the original work, code p is used."

To summarize, if there are two dates, and the original was a motion picture but you are cataloging the video copy, you would use "c" if the earlier date is the original copyright date, "p" if the earlier date is the production date. If using "c" the information should be in area 4:

    1990, c1945.

If using "p" the earlier date would be in the note that gives information about the original production.

    Originally produced as motion picture by United Artists in
    1972.

"Dat tp" "r" would not be used for these examples because a change in form is involved, from film to video.

"MEBE"

"MEBE" will disappear from the fixed field some time in 1991 as the first step in format integration.

INTERACTIVE VIDEO

Laser technology makes it possible for videodiscs to contain copies of motion pictures, still pictures, music, text, spoken material, and computer files. Computer technology allows this material to be indexed, accessed in any order, and played back, displayed, edited and/or printed out as desired. This interaction of a user with the contents of a videodisc, using a computer, is referred to as "interactive video."

Videodisc producers have devised a system of guidelines that defines five levels of interactivity.

Level-O discs are the equivalent of pre-recorded videocassettes. There is no interaction with the contents.

Level-I discs may be searched by chapters (sections of the disc) or by individual frame. The producer of the disc can program it to stop at selected points during playback.

Level-II discs require microprocessor-equipped players. Discs may be pre-programmed by the producer, or may be programmed by the user who is "interacting" with the material on the disc. Programming may include continuous loops, or timed loops, of some of the program material. Codes are not standardized within the industry, requiring different codes for different players.

Level-III discs require an external computer that becomes a programmable controller for the videodisc player. The discs contain no pre-programmed codes; all is done in an interactive fashion. There are many systems available now to take advantage of this technology.

Level-IV discs contain computer files in addition to the audiovisual information. This level, only recently added, is being developed.

Terminology

Interactive videodisc systems are also referred to in the current literature as hypermedia and as multimedia.

Background

There are two types of laser videodiscs. (An earlier videodisc system, the CED disc, used a stylus for playback). Both laser discs use analog signals, not digital. Development of digital interactive systems is underway by Philips, using the standard compact disc format.

One type of laser videodisc is referred to as CLV (constant linear velocity). These CLV discs allow 60 minutes of playing time per side, but, while some can be searched by individual frame, the image displayed is not as high quality as that displayed by a CAV disc. CLV discs are not suitable for true interactive purposes.

The other type of laser videodisc is referred to as CAV (constant angular velocity). These CAV discs contain up to 54,000 frames per side, or 30 minutes of playing time. Each frame uses one track, and the player can be programmed to select one frame for display as a still image for any length of time. These are the videodiscs used in all interactive systems.

Examples

Lions of the African Night, a 60-minute film by the National Geographic Society, is an example of a level-O videodisc. It is played continuously.

The National Gallery of Art has produced a videodisc including a 22-minute segment on the history of the National Gallery, a 27-minute tour of the gallery, and 3353 frames that show 1645 items in the collection, each with a frame containing information about the artist and the work. This level-I disc uses random access, slow motion, freeze frames, and chapter search as interactive features.

An example of a level-III package is *The '88 Vote,* produced by ABC News Interactive, and distributed by Optical Data Corp. It includes a two-sided videodisc, a HyperCard stack (for use on a Macintosh computer), printed curriculum guides, and support material. The video includes footage from the 1988 presidential campaign, including portions of debates and press conferences. One audio channel contains the live sound, the other commentary by an ABC correspondent. Text is displayed on the computer screen through HyperCard. Users can create their own documentaries. Other titles from ABC News include *In the Holy Land* and *The Great Quake of '89.*

Interactive systems have been designed for the IBM PC or PS/2, the Commodore Amiga, the Apple Macintosh, and the Apple IIGS.

Cataloging

Levels O, I, and II are cataloged as videorecordings. The purchaser receives a videodisc and perhaps some written material. The only hardware needed is the videodisc player with monitor, cables, etc. The level II disc needs a special player. Sony and Pioneer discs are not interchangeable.

The levels III and IV discs usually come with computer files on their own carriers and need a computer connected to the videodisc player. The contents of the videodisc is being displayed, edited, and/or used in some fashion with the aid of the computer program, and some text may come from the computer file.

Some new types of material include pictures, sound, text, and computer files all on one compact disc. A special player is required for use. There is discussion at the national level about what to call these and how to catalog them. There have been suggestions to treat them as videorecordings with accompanying materials. Others suggest they be treated as kits, or that new rules be developed.

THE EXAMPLES

The 40 examples that follow include all types of motion pictures and videorecordings. Information has been transcribed from title and credits screens. Only the information most important for cataloging was transcribed. In some cases information from the container is reproduced and/or transcribed as well.

Most of these examples are for videorecordings, many of which are video copies of films. Cataloging of motion pictures varies only in the GMD and in area 5 from the video cataloging.

EXAMPLES

Example 1

Title screens

Touchstone Pictures
and
Amblin Entertainment
in association with
Silver Screen Partners III
present
Who Framed
Roger Rabbit?
Directed by
Robert Zemeckis
Screenplay by
Jeffrey Price
&
Peter S. Seaman
Produced by
Robert Watts
&
Frank Marshall
Starring
Bob Hoskins
Christopher Lloyd
Executive Producers
Steven Spielberg
&
Kathleen Kennedy
Director of Animation
Richard Williams

From the back of container

Amblin	Touchstone
Entertainment	Home Video

Example 1

```
Who framed Roger Rabbit? [videorecording] / Touchstone Pictures and
    Amblin Entertainment in association with Silver Screen Partners
    III ; directed by Robert Zemeckis ; produced by Robert Watts &
    Frank Marshall ; screenplay by Jeffrey Price & Peter S. Seaman ;
    executive producers, Steven Spielberg & Kathleen Kennedy ; direc-
    tor of animation, Richard Williams. -- [Burbank, CA : Touchstone
    Home Video ; distributed by Buena Vista Home Video], 1989.
        1 videocassette (106 min.) : sd., col. ; 1/2 in.

        VHS.
        Closed-captioned for the hearing impaired.
        Cast: Bob Hoskins, Christopher Lloyd, Joanna Cassidy, Charles
    Fleischer (voice of Roger Rabbit), Kathleen Turner (voice of
    Jessica Rabbit), Stubby Kaye, Alan Tilvern.
        Credits: Music, Alan Silvestri ; special visual effects, Indus-
    trial Light & Magic.
        Based on: Who censored Roger Rabbit? / by Gary K. Wolf.
        Originally produced as motion picture in 1989.
        Rated PG.
        Summary: A tale of a man, a woman, and a rabbit in a triangle
    of trouble, in a world where people and Toons (cartoon characters)
    live side by side.

        1. Feature films.  2. Animated films.  3. Comedy films.  4.
    Films for the hearing impaired.  5. Rabbit, Roger (Fictitious
    character)  6. Rabbit, Jessica (Fictitious character) I. Zemeckis,
    Robert, 1952-  II. Watts, Robert.  III. Marshall, Frank.  IV.
    Price, Jeffrey.  V. Seaman, Peter S.  VI. Spielberg, Steven.  VII.
    Kennedy, Kathleen.  VIII. Williams, Richard.  IX. Silvestri, Alan.
    X. Hoskins, Bob.  XI. Lloyd, Christopher.  XII. Cassidy, Joanna.
    XIII. Fleischer, Charles.  XIV. Turner, Kathleen, 1954-  XV.
    Kaye, Stubby.  XVI. Tilvern, Alan.  XVII. Wolf, Gary K.  Who
    censored Roger Rabbit? XVIII. Touchstone Pictures.  XIX. Amblin
    Entertainment, Inc.  XX. Silver Screen Partners III.  XXI. Touch-
    stone Home Video.  XXII. Industrial Light & Magic.

PN1995.9.C55
791.43617
```

Animation is important in this film, so I chose to list the director of animation in the statement of responsibility rather than in the notes. Note the statement of responsibility is transcribed exactly as the information is found in the credits, including the use of the ampersand; the same type of information given in the formal notes (Cast, Credits) is presented in a formal style rather than as an exact transcription.

Rule numbers for notes: 7.7B10f, 7.7B2, 7.7B6a, 7.7B6b, 7.7B7, 7.7B9, 7.7B14, 7.7B17. "VHS" is moved into the first position in this example.

Note the distribution information from the container.

Example 1

```
Type: g      Bib lvl: m Source: d    Lang: eng
Type mat: v  Enc lvl: I Govt pub:    Ctry: cau
Int lvl: g   Mod rec:   Tech: c      Leng: 106
Accomp:      MEBE: 0    Dat tp: s    Dates: 1989,
Desc: a
  1   010
  2   040      XXX ‡c XXX
  3   007      v ‡b f ‡d c ‡e b ‡f a ‡g h ‡h o ‡i s
  4   090      PN1995.9.C55
  5   092      791.43617 ‡2 20
  6   049      XXXX
  7   245 00   Who framed Roger Rabbit? ‡h videorecording / ‡c Touchstone
Pictures and Amblin Entertainment in association with Silver Screen
Partners III ; directed by Robert Zemeckis ; produced by Robert Watts &
Frank Marshall ; screenplay by Jeffrey Price & Peter S. Seaman ; execu-
tive producers, Steven Spielberg & Kathleen Kennedy ; director of anima-
tion, Richard Williams.
  8   260      [Burbank, CA : ‡b Touchstone Home Video ; ‡b distributed by
Buena Vista Home Video], ‡c 1989.
  9   300      1 videocassette (106 min.) : ‡b sd., col. ; ‡c 1/2 in.
 10   538      VHS.
 12   500      Closed-captioned for the hearing impaired.
 13   511 1    Bob Hoskins, Christopher Lloyd, Joanna Cassidy, Charles
Fleischer (voice of Roger Rabbit), Kathleen Turner (voice of Jessica
Rabbit), Stubby Kaye, Alan Tilvern.
 14   508      Music, Alan Silvestri ; special visual effects, Industrial
Light & Magic.
 15   500      Based on: Who censored Roger Rabbit? / by Gary K. Wolf.
 16   500      Originally produced as motion picture in 1989.
 17   500      Rated PG.
 18   520      A tale of a man, a woman, and a rabbit in a triangle of
trouble, in a world where people and Toons (cartoon characters) live
side by side.
 19   650 0    Feature films.
 20   650 0    Animated films.
 21   650 0    Comedy films.
 21   650 0    Films for the hearing impaired.
 22   650 0    Rabbit, Roger (Fictitious character)
 23   650 0    Rabbit, Jessica (Fictitious character)
 24   700 11   Zemeckis, Robert, ‡d 1952-
 25   700 11   Watts, Robert.
 26   700 11   Marshall, Frank.
 27   700 11   Price, Jeffrey.
 28   700 11   Seaman, Peter S.
 29   700 11   Spielberg, Steven.
 30   700 11   Kennedy, Kathleen.
 31   700 11   Williams, Richard.
 32   700 11   Silvestri, Alan.
 33   700 11   Hoskins, Bob.
 34   700 11   Lloyd, Christopher.
 35   700 11   Cassidy, Joanna.
 36   700 11   Fleischer, Charles.
```
(Continued next page)

Example 1

```
37   700 11   Turner, Kathleen, 1954-
38   700 11   Kaye, Stubby.
39   700 11   Tilvern, Alan.
40   700 11   Wolf, Gary K. ‡t Who censored Roger Rabbit?
41   710 21   Touchstone Pictures.
42   710 21   Amblin Entertainment, Inc.
43   710 21   Silver Screen Partners III.
44   710 21   Touchstone Home Video.
45   710 21   Industrial Light & Magic.
```

ACCESS FOR FICTIONAL CHARACTERS

There are no provisions in *AACR 2* for making access points under the names of fictional characters. If it is desirable to provide access under such names, one must follow the instructions in the Library of Congress *Subject Cataloging Manual: Subject Headings*, section H 1610 (and, in this case, section H 1430). It can be debated whether "Rabbit" is a surname in this case. One could equally well have entered both names in direct order, "Roger Rabbit (Fictitious character)" and "Jessica Rabbit (Fictitious character)". In either case, references would be made from the form not chosen to guide users who might look under the variant form from that form to the established form.

Example 2

Title screens

Crown Video presents
Crown Movie Classics
Liberty Films
An RKO Radio Release
Frank Capra's
It's a wonderful life
James Stewart
Donna Reed
Lionel Barrymore
Thomas Mitchell
Henry Travers
Musical Score
Written and Directed by Dimitri Tiomkin
Produced and Directed by Frank Capra
© MCMXLVI

From back of container

IT'S A WONDERFUL LIFE

1946

JAMES STEWART
DONNA REED
LIONEL BARRYMORE
BEULAH BONDI
Directed by
FRANK CAPRA

Frank Capra's feel-good classic about a
despondent young man who decides to
end it all, only to have a change of heart
after a visit from a bumbling angel who
is trying to earn his wings. Stewart
earned his first Academy Award
nomination for his memorable role as
the man who gerts to see what his town
would have been like if he hand never
been born. One of the most engaging
and heartwarming films of all time.
Black & white. 130 min.

IT'S A WONDERFUL LIFE • VHS • 876825
CROWN VIDEO, ONE PARK AVENUE, NEW YORK, NY 10016

CROWN M⊗VIE CLASSICS™

Example 2

```
It's a wonderful life (Motion picture)
    Frank Capra's It's a wonderful life [videorecording] / Liberty
Films ; produced and directed by Frank Capra ; screenplay by Frances
Goodrich, Albert Hackett, Frank Capra. -- [New York, N.Y.] : Crown
Video, [198-?], c1946.
    1 videocassette (130 min.) : sd., b&w ; 1/2 in. -- (Crown movie
classics)

    Cast: James Stewart, Donna Reed, Lionel Barrymore, Thomas
Mitchell, Henry Travers.
    "Musical score written and directed by Dimitri Tiomkin."
    "An RKO Radio release."
    Originally produced as motion picture in 1946.
    VHS.
    Summary: Sentimental story about a discouraged businessman's
(James Stewart) re-evaluation of the significance of his life. A
fumbling guardian angel struggles to prevent Stewart's suicide by
convincing him of his importance to his small home town, showing him
what it would be like if he had never been born.

    1. Feature films. 2. Christmas films. I. Capra, Frank, 1897-
II. Goodrich, Frances. III. Hackett, Albert. IV. Stewart, James,
1908- V. Reed, Donna, 1921-1986. VI. Barrymore, Lionel, 1878-1954.
VII. Mitchell, Thomas, 1892-1962. VIII. Travers, Henry, 1874-1965.
IX. Tiomkin, Dimitri. X. Liberty Films. XI. Crown Video. XII
Series.

PN1995.9.C5
791.436353
```

According to an LC rule interpretation, the personal name in the possessive form appearing before the title is to be retained as part of the title proper. The "actual title" is then used as a uniform title main entry because the "the title of the work is obscured by the wording of the title proper" (25.2A4). The words "motion picture" in parentheses are used as a qualifier for the uniform title. This is not a GMD.

This is the original black-and-white version of this film, not the colorized version. The color version would have a uniform title including something about the version (see Example 3).

There is no period after [198-?] as the bracket or closing parenthesis serves as closing punctuation for areas 4, 5, and 6, according to LCRI 1.0C (*CSB* 45).

The first date in area 4 is given as shown as no date appeared on the film label or container except the original copyright date of 1946. The videocassette is assumed to have been published and/or distributed sometime in the 1980s.

The series information is not bracketed because it appears on the title/credits frames.

Rule numbers for notes: 7.7B6a, 7.7B6b, 7.7B9, 7.7B9, 7.7B10f, 7.7B17.

OCLC comment

"Ctry" is coded for California where this film was originally produced, rather than for New York, the place where the distributor is located.

Example 2

```
Type: g      Bib lvl: m Source: d   Lang: eng
Type mat: v Enc lvl: I Govt pub:    Ctry: cau
Int lvl: g  Mod rec:   Tech: c      Leng: 130
Accomp:     MEBE: 0     Dat tp: c   Dates: 1980,1946
Desc: a
 1   010
 2   040      XXX ǂc XXX
 3   007      v ǂb f ǂd b ǂe b ǂf a ǂg h ǂh o ǂi m
 4   090      PN1995.9.C5
 5   092      791.436353 ǂ2 20
 6   049      XXXX
 7   130 0    It's a wonderful life (Motion picture)
 8   245 00 Frank Capra's It's a wonderful life ǂh videorecording / ǂc
Liberty Films ; produced and directed by Frank Capra ; screenplay by
Frances Goodrich, Albert Hackett, Frank Capra.
 9   260      [New York, N.Y.] : ǂb Crown Video, ǂc [198-?], c1946.
10   300      1 videocassette (130 min.) : ǂb sd., b&w ; ǂc 1/2 in.
11   440   0 Crown movie classics
12   511 1   James Stewart, Donna Reed, Lionel Barrymore, Thomas
Mitchell, Henry Travers.
13   500      "Musical score written and directed by Dimitri Tiomkin."
14   500      "An RKO Radio release."
15   500      Originally produced as motion picture in 1946.
16   538      VHS.
17   520      Sentimental story about a discouraged businessman's (James
Stewart) re-evaluation of the significance of his life.  A fumbling
guardian angel struggles to prevent Stewart's suicide by convincing him
of his importance to his small home town, showing him what it would be
like if he had never been born.
18   650   0 Feature films.
19   650   0 Christmas films.
20   700 11 Capra, Frank, ǂd 1897-
21   700 11 Goodrich, Frances.
22   700 11 Hackett, Albert.
23   700 11 Stewart, James, ǂd 1908-
24   700 11 Reed, Donna, ǂd 1921-1986.
25   700 11 Barrymore, Lionel, ǂd 1878-1954.
26   700 11 Mitchell, Thomas, ǂd 1892-1962.
27   700 11 Travers, Henry, ǂd 1874-1965.
28   700 11 Tiomkin, Dimitri.
29   710 21 Liberty Films.
30   710 21 Crown Video.
```

Example 3

Title screens

Warner Bros. Pictures
The Vitaphone Corp.
present
42nd Street
Directed by Lloyd Bacon
Dances and ensembles created and staged by
Busby Berkeley
Words and music by
Al Dubin and Harry Warren
Screen play by
Rian James and James Seymour
based on the novel by Bradford Ropes
...
Warner Baxter
Bebe Daniels
George Brent
Ruby Keeler
Guy Kibbee
Una Merkel
Ginger Rogers
Ned Sparks
Dick Powell

[at end of film]
color version copyright Turner 1986
stereo conversion by Chace Productions
color system color conversion by Technology Inc.
CBS/Fox Video

Cassette label

Example 3

```
42nd Street (Motion picture : Color version)
    42nd Street [videorecording] / Warner Bros. Pictures ; directed by
Lloyd Bacon ; screen play by Rian James and James Seymour. -- Color
version. -- [Livonia, Mich.] : CBS/Fox Video, c1986.
    1 videocassette (89 min.) : sd., col. ; 1/2 in.

    Title on cassette label: 42nd Street in color.
    Cast: Warner Baxter, Bebe Daniels, George Brent, Ruby Keeler, Guy
Kibbee, Una Merkel, Ginger Rogers, Ned Sparks, Dick Powell.
    "Dances and ensembles created and staged by Busby Berkeley. Words
and music by Al Dubin and Harry Warren."
    Originally issued as black-and-white motion picture in 1933.
    VHS hi-fi.
    Summary: Classic plot involves a tyrannical director, egotistical
leading lady, and wide-eyed ingenue.


    1. Musical films.  2. Feature films.  I. Bacon, Lloyd, 1890-1955.
II. James, Rian, 1899-  III. Seymour, James.  IV. Baxter, Warner,
1889-1951.  V. Daniels, Bebe, 1901-1971.  VI. Brent, George, 1904-
1979.  VII. Keeler, Ruby.  VIII. Kibbee, Guy, 1882-1956.  IX. Merkel,
Una, 1903-  X. Rogers, Ginger, 1911-  XI. Sparks, Ned, 1883-1957.
XII. Powell, Dick, 1904-1963.  XIII. Berkeley, Busby, 1895-  XIV.
Dubin, Al.  XV. Warren, Harry, 1893-  XVI. Warner Bros. Pictures.
XVII. CBS/Fox Video.  XVIII. Title: Forty-Second Street. XIX. Title:
42nd Street in color.

PN1995.9.M86
791.437
```

This is a colorized version of a black-and-white film. The uniform title main entry is needed because there are at least two works with the same title, the b&w version, and the color version. We are assuming this title was needed as an added entry, causing a uniform title to be constructed and used for all instances of the work. If there is no conflict in your catalog, or no need for an added entry for this work, you could avoid using the uniform title main entry.

The date used in area 4 is that given at the end of the film, the copyright date for the color version.

The edtion information is not bracketed because it does appear on the title/credits frames.

Rule numbers for notes: 7.7B4, 7.7B6a, 7.7B6b, 7.7B7, 7.7B10f, 7.7B17.

36

Example 3

```
Type: g       Bib lvl: m Source: d    Lang: eng
Type mat: v Enc lvl: I Govt pub:      Ctry: cau
Int lvl:      Mod rec:   Tech: l      Leng: 089
Accomp:       MEBE: 0    Dat tp: s    Dates: 1986,
Desc: a
  1   010
  2   040       XXX ǂc XXX
  3   007       v ǂb f ǂd c ǂe b ǂf a ǂg h ǂh o ǂi s
  4   090       PN1995.9.M86

  5   092       791.437 ǂ2 20
  6   049       XXXX
  7   130 0     42nd Street (Motion picture : Color version)
  8   245 00    42nd Street ǂh videorecording / ǂc Warner Bros. Pictures ;
directed by Lloyd Bacon ; screen play by Rian James and James Seymour.
  9   250       Color version.
 10   260       [Livonia, Mich.] : ǂb CBS/Fox Video, ǂc c1986.
 11   300       1 videocassette (89 min.) : ǂb sd., col. ; ǂc 1/2 in.
 12   500       Title on cassette label: 42nd Street in color.
 13   511 1     Warner Baxter, Bebe Daniels, George Brent, Ruby Keeler, Guy
Kibbee, Una Merkel, Ginger Rogers, Ned Sparks, Dick Powell.
 14   500       "Dances and ensembles created and staged by Busby Berkeley.
Words and music by Al Dubin and Harry Warren."
 15   500       Originally issued as black-and-white motion picture in
1933.
 16   538       VHS hi-fi.
 17   520       Classic plot involves a tyrannical director, egotistical
leading lady, and wide-eyed ingenue.
 18   650 0  Musical films.
 19   650 0  Feature films.
 20   700 11 Bacon, Lloyd, ǂd 1890-1955.
 21   700 11 James, Rian, ǂd 1899-
 22   700 11 Seymour, James.
 23   700 11 Baxter, Warner, ǂd 1889-1951.
 24   700 11 Daniels, Bebe, ǂd 1901-1971.
 25   700 11 Brent, George, ǂd 1904-1979.
 26   700 11 Keeler, Ruby.
 27   700 11 Kibbee, Guy, ǂd 1882-1956.
 28   700 11 Merkel, Una, ǂd 1903-
 29   700 11 Rogers, Ginger, ǂd 1911-
 30   700 11 Sparks, Ned, ǂd 1883-1957.
 31   700 11 Powell, Dick, ǂd 1904-1963.
 32   700 11 Berkeley, Busby, ǂd 1895-
 33   700 11 Dubin, Al.
 34   700 11 Warren, Harry, ǂd 1893-
 35   710 21 Warner Bros. Pictures.
 36   710 21 CBS/Fox Video.
 37   740 01 Forty-Second Street.
 38   740 01 42nd Street in color.
```

"Dat tp" here is "s". The color version is a new work.

Example 4

Title screens

MGM/UA Home Video

————————

Metro-Goldwyn-Mayer
presents
Cary Grant
Katharine Hepburn
James Stewart
in
The
Philadelphia Story
with
Ruth Hussey
Screen Play by
Donald Ogden Stewart
Based on the Play by
Philip Barry
Produced by the Theatre Guild, Inc.
produced by
Joseph L. Mankiewicz
directed by
George Cukor

```
The Philadelphia story [videorecording] / Metro-Goldwyn-Mayer ;
    produced by Joseph L. Mankiewicz ; directed by George Cukor ;
    screen play by Donald Ogden Stewart. -- [New York] : MGM/UA Home
    Video, [1983]
        1 videocassette (112 min.) : sd., b&w ; 1/2 in.

    Cast: Cary Grant, Katharine Hepburn, James Stewart, Ruth
Hussey.
    Based on the play by Philip Barry.
    Originally produced as motion picture in 1940.
    VHS.
    Summary: Sophisticated romantic comedy about a rich, spoiled
socialite who learns some things about who she is and what she
really wants on the eve of her second marriage.

    1. Comedy films. 2. Feature films. I. Mankiewicz, Joseph L.
II. Cukor, George Dewey, 1899-  III. Stewart, Donald Ogden, 1894-
IV. Grant, Cary, 1904-  V. Hepburn, Katharine, 1909-  VI. Stewart,
James, 1908-  VII. Hussey, Ruth, 1917-  VIII. Barry, Philip, 1896-
1949. Philadelphia story.  IX. Metro-Goldwyn-Mayer.  X. MGM/UA
Home Video.

PN1995.9.M3
791.436
```

Example 4

Examples 4 and 5 represent two film versions of the same play.
Rule numbers for notes: 7.7B6a, 7.7B7, 7.7B7, 7.7B10f, 7.7B17.
The date of 1983 is given on the container as the copyright date of the package. This is bracketed in area 4 as the assumed date of publication of the item.

```
Type: g      Bib lvl: m Source: d    Lang: eng
Type mat: v  Enc lvl: I Govt pub:    Ctry: cau
Int lvl: g   Mod rec:   Tech: l      Leng: 112
Accomp:      MEBE: 0    Dat tp: p    Dates: 1983,1940
Desc: a
 1   010
 2   040      XXX ‡c XXX
 3   007      v ‡b f ‡d b ‡e b ‡f a ‡g h ‡h o ‡i m
 4   090      PN1995.9.M3
 5   092      791.436 ‡2 20
 6   049      XXXX
 7   245 04   The Philadelphia story ‡h videorecording / ‡c Metro-
Goldwyn-Mayer ; produced by Joseph L. Mankiewicz ; directed by George
Cukor ; screen play by Donald Ogden Stewart.
 8   260      [New York] : ‡b MGM/UA Home Video, ‡c [1983]
 9   300      1 videocassette (112 min.) : ‡b sd., b&w ; ‡c 1/2 in.
10   511 1    Cary Grant, Katharine Hepburn, James Stewart, Ruth Hussey.
11   500      Based on the play by Philip Barry.
12   500      Originally produced as motion picture in 1940.
13   538      VHS.
14   520      Sophisticated romantic comedy about a rich, spoiled social-
ite who learns some things about who she is and what she really wants on
the eve of her second marriage.
15   650  0   Comedy films.
16   650  0   Feature films.
17   700 11   Mankiewicz, Joseph L.
18   700 11   Cukor, George Dewey, ‡d 1899-
19   700 11   Stewart, Donald Ogden, ‡d 1894-
20   700 11   Grant, Cary, ‡d 1904-
21   700 11   Hepburn, Katharine, ‡d 1909-
22   700 11   Stewart, James, ‡d 1908-
23   700 11   Hussey, Ruth, ‡d 1917-
24   700 11   Barry, Philip, ‡d 1896-1949. ‡t Philadelphia story.
25   710 21   Metro-Goldwyn-Mayer.
26   710 21   MGM/UA Home Video.
```

"Dat tp" is coded "p" for this example. The work is identical to that previously issued except for form, and both dates are known.

Example 5

Title screens

MGM/UA Home Video
—————

Metro Goldwyn Mayer
presents
in
VistaVision
A
Sol C. Siegel
presentation
starring
Bing Crosby
Grace Kelly
Frank Sinatra
in

High

Society

also starring
Celeste Holm
John Lund
Louis Calhern
Sidney Blackmer
and
Louis Armstrong
and his band
Screen Play by
John Patrick
based on a play by
Philip Barry
Music & Lyrics by
Cole Porter
Music supervised &
adapted by
Johnny Green
and
Saul Chaplin
directed by
Charles Walters

Example 5

```
High society [videorecording] / Metro Goldwyn Mayer ; directed by
    Charles Walters ; screen play by John Patrick. -- [New York] :
    MGM/UA Home Video, [1988]
        1 videocassette (107 min.) : sd., col. ; 1/2 in.

        Cast: Bing Crosby, Grace Kelly, Frank Sinatra, Celeste Holm,
    John Lund, Louis Calhern, Sidney Blackmer, Louis Armstrong and his
    band.
        "Music & lyrics by Cole Porter. Music supervised & adapted by
    Johnny Green and Saul Chaplin."
        "A Sol C. Siegel presentation."
        Based on: The Philadelphia story / by Philip Barry.
        Originally produced as motion picture in 1956; remake of 1940
    film, The Philadelphia story.
        VHS hi-fi.
        Summary: A sophisticated comedy with music. Preparations for
    the wedding of a headstrong society divorcee to a priggish self-
    made man are interrupted on the eve of the ceremony by the bride's
    easy-going ex-husband and a debonair reporter from a gossip maga-
    zine.

        1. Comedy films.  2. Musical films. 3. Feature films.  I.
    Walters, Charles, 1911-  II. Patrick, John.  III. Crosby, Bing,
    1904-1977.  IV. Grace, Princess of Monaco, 1929-1982.  V. Sinatra,
    Frank, 1915-  VI. Holm, Celeste, 1919-  VII. Lund, John, 1913-
    VIII. Calhern, Louis, 1895-1956.  IX.  Blackmer, Sidney, 1895-
    1973.  X. Armstrong, Louis, 1900-1971.  XI.  Porter, Cole, 1891-
    1964.  XII. Green, Johnny.  XIII. Chaplin, Saul.  XIV. Siegel, Sol
    C., 1903-1982.  XV.  Barry, Philip, 1896-1949.  Philadelphia
    story.  XVI. Metro-Goldwyn-Mayer.  XVII. MGM/UA Home Video.

PN1995.9.M3
791.436
```

In the credits for this film Metro-Goldwyn-Mayer is shown without the hypens. They weren't consistent in their use of hyphens in their own corporate name. The correct form of the added entry includes the hyphens.
Rule numbers for notes: 7.7B6a, 7.7B6b, 7.7B6b, 7.7B7, 7.7B7, 7.7B10f, 7.7B17.
On the package:
Package design © 1988 Turner Entertainment Co.
This date is used in area 4 as the assumed date of publication/distribution of this video.

Example 5

```
Type: g      Bib lvl: m Source: d    Lang: eng
Type mat: v  Enc lvl: I Govt pub:    Ctry: cau
Int lvl: g   Mod rec:   Tech: l      Leng: 107
Accomp:      MEBE: 0    Dat tp: p    Dates: 1988,1956
Desc: a
 1    010
 2    040      XXX ‡c XXX
 3    007      v ‡b f ‡d c ‡e b ‡f a ‡g h ‡h o ‡i m
 4    090      PN1995.9.M3
 5    092      791.436 ‡2 20
 6    049      XXXX
 7    245 00   High society ‡h videorecording / ‡c Metro Goldwyn Mayer ;
directed by Charles Walters ; screen play by John Patrick.
 8    260      [New York] : ‡b MGM/UA Home Video, ‡c [1988]
 9    300      1 videocassette (107 min.) : ‡b sd., col. ; ‡c 1/2 in.
10    511 1    Bing Crosby, Grace Kelly, Frank Sinatra, Celeste Holm, John
Lund, Louis Calhern, Sidney Blackmer, Louis Armstrong and his band.
11    500      "Music & lyrics by Cole Porter. Music supervised & adapted
by Johnny Green and Saul Chaplin."
12    500      "A Sol C. Siegel presentation."
13    500      Based on: The Philadelphia story / by Philip Barry.
14    500      Originally produced as motion picture in 1956; remake of
1940 film, The Philadelphia story.
15    538      VHS hi-fi.
16    520      A sophisticated comedy with music. Preparations for the
wedding of a headstrong society divorcee to a priggish self-made man are
interrupted on the eve of the ceremony by the bride's easy-going ex-
husband and a debonair reporter from a gossip magazine.
17    650 0    Comedy films.
18    650 0    Musical films.
19    650 0    Feature films.
20    700 11   Walters, Charles, ‡d 1911-
21    700 11   Patrick, John.
22    700 11   Crosby, Bing, ‡d 1904-1977.
23    700 01   Grace, ‡c Princess of Monaco, ‡d 1929-1982.
24    700 11   Sinatra, Frank, ‡d 1915-
25    700 11   Holm, Celeste, ‡d 1919-
26    700 11   Lund, John, ‡d 1913-
27    700 11   Calhern, Louis, ‡d 1895-1956.
28    700 11   Blackmer, Sidney, ‡d 1895-1973.
29    700 11   Armstrong, Louis, ‡d 1900-1971.
30    700 11   Porter, Cole, ‡d 1891-1964.
31    700 11   Green, Johnny.
32    700 11   Chaplin, Saul.
33    700 11   Siegel, Sol C., ‡d 1903-1982.
34    700 11   Barry, Philip, ‡d 1896-1949. ‡t Philadelphia story.
35    710 21   Metro-Goldwyn-Mayer.
36    710 21   MGM/UA Home Video.
```

42

Example 6

Title screens

A
Paramount Picture
Irving Berlin's
Holiday Inn
A
Mark Sandrich Production
Starring
Bing Crosby
and
Fred Astaire
with
Marjorie Reynolds
Virginia Dale
Walter Abel
Louise Beavers
Screen Play by Claude Binyon
Adaptation by Elmer Rice
Based on an idea by
Irving Berlin
Lyrics and Music by
Irving Berlin
Produced and Directed by
Mark Sandrich

On container:

Example 6

```
Holiday Inn (Motion picture)
   Irving Berlin's Holiday Inn [videorecording] / a Paramount picture
; produced and directed by Mark Sandrich ; screen play by Claude
Binyon ; adaptation by Elmer Rice ; lyrics and music by Irving Ber-
lin. -- [Universal City, CA : MCA Videocassette, 1981]
   1 videocassette (101 min.) : sd., b&w ; 1/2 in.

   Cast: Bing Crosby, Fred Astaire, Marjorie Reynolds, Virginia Dale,
Walter Abel, Louise Beavers.
   "Based on an idea by Irving Berlin."
   Originally produced as motion picture in 1942.
   VHS.
   Summary: A former song and dance man with an inn in New England is
saved from financial disaster and a forlorn Christmas by the showman-
ship of old friends.

   1. Feature films.  2. Musical films.  3. Christmas films.  I.
Sandrich, Mark, 1900-1945.  II. Binyon, Claude, 1905-1978.  III.
Rice, Elmer L., 1892-1967.  IV. Berlin, Irving, 1888-  V. Crosby,
Bing, 1904-1977.  VI.  Astaire, Fred.  VII. Reynolds, Marjorie.
VIII. Dale, Virginia.  IX. Abel, Walter, 1898-1987.  X. Beavers,
Louise, 1902-1962.  XI. Paramount Pictures, inc.  XII. MCA Videocas-
sette.

PN1995.9.M86
791.43633
```

Rule numbers for notes: 7.7B6a, 7.7B7, 7.7B7, 7.7B10f, 7.7B17.
    The uniform title main entry is used here because the title proper includes words preceding the "actual" title. A title added entry for "Holiday Inn" could be used instead of the uniform title main entry.

44

Example 6

```
Type: g       Bib lvl: m Source: d   Lang: eng
Type mat: v Enc lvl: I Govt pub:    Ctry: cau
Int lvl: g  Mod rec:   Tech: l      Leng: 101
Accomp:     MEBE: 0    Dat tp: p    Dates: 1981,1942
Desc: a
 1   010
 2   040      XXX ǂc XXX
 3   007      v ǂb f ǂd b ǂe b ǂf a ǂg h ǂh o ǂi m
 4   090      PN1995.9.M86
 5   092      791.43633 ǂ2 20
 6   049      XXXX
 7   130 0    Holiday Inn (Motion picture)
 8   245 00   Irving Berlin's Holiday Inn ǂh videorecording / ǂc a Para-
mount picture ; produced and directed by Mark Sandrich ; screen play by
Claude Binyon ; adaptation by Elmer Rice ; lyrics and music by Irving
Berlin.
 9   260      [Universal City, CA : ǂb MCA Videocassette, ǂc 1981]
10   300      1 videocassette (101 min.) : ǂb sd., b&w ; ǂc 1/2 in.
11   511 1    Bing Crosby, Fred Astaire, Marjorie Reynolds, Virginia
Dale, Walter Abel, Louise Beavers.
12   500      "Based on an idea by Irving Berlin."
13   500      Originally produced as motion picture in 1942.
14   538      VHS.
15   520      A former song and dance man with an inn in New England is
saved from financial disaster and a forlorn Christmas by the showmanship
of old friends.
16   650  0   Feature films.
17   650  0   Musical films.
18   650  0   Christmas films.
19   700 11   Sandrich, Mark, ǂd 1900-1945.
20   700 11   Binyon, Claude, ǂd 1905-1978.
21   700 11   Rice, Elmer L., ǂd 1892-1967.
22   700 11   Berlin, Irving, ǂd 1888-
23   700 11   Crosby, Bing, ǂd 1904-1977.
24   700 11   Astaire, Fred.
25   700 11   Reynolds, Marjorie.
26   700 11   Dale, Virginia.
27   700 11   Abel, Walter, ǂd 1898-1987.
28   700 11   Beavers, Louise, ǂd 1902-1962.
29   710 21   Paramount Pictures, Inc.
30   710 21   MCA Videocassette.
```

Example 7

Title screens

United Artists

A film produced by Marcello Danon

Ugo Tognazzi

Michel Serrault in

Birds of a Feather

based on the play La Cage aux Folles by Jean Poiret

*screenplay by Francis Veber, Edouard Molinaro,
Marcello Danon, Jean Poiret*

Director of photography, Armando Nannuzzi

*Music composed and conducted by the maestro,
Ennio Morricone*

Directed by Edouard Molinaro

Example 7

```
Cage aux folles (Motion picture).  English.
   Birds of a feather [videorecording] : a film / produced by
Marcello Danon ; directed by Edouard Molinaro. -- [Farmington Hills,
MI : Magnetic Video, 1981]
   1 videocassette (91 min.) : sd., col. ; 1/2 in.

   Dubbed into English.
   Title on container: La cage aux folles = Birds of a feather.
   Cast: Ugo Tognazzi, Michel Serrault, Carmen Scarpitta, Remi
Laurent, Benny Luke, Luisa Maneri, Michel Galabru.
   Credits: Screenplay, Francis Veber, Edouard Molinaro, Marcello
Danon, Jean Poiret ; music, Ennio Morricone ; director of photogra-
phy, Armando Nannuzzi.
   Based on: La cage aux folles / Jean Poiret.
   A co-production of Les Productions artistes associés and Da Ma
produzione SPA, originally produced as French-Italian motion picture
in 1979. Released in the United States by United Artists.
   VHS.
   Rating: R.
   Summary: A farce involving a flamboyant homosexual couple's at-
tempt to appear to be conventional parents in front of the prospec-
tive in-laws of the son of one of the men.
   "MC: 4506-30."

   1. Feature films.  I. Danon, Marcello.  II. Molinaro, Edouard.
III. Tognazzi, Ugo.  IV. Serrault, Michel, 1928-  V. Poiret, Jean,
1926-  Cage aux folles.  VI. Productions artistes associés.  VII. Da
Ma produzione, S.P.A.  VIII. Magnetic Video.  IX. Title.

PQ2631.O (number for Poiret)
PN1995.9.F4 (number as feature film)
791.436353
```

This example is a foreign film dubbed into English. The uniform title used as main entry is the original French title for the film, with the language into which it has been dubbed added as directed in 25.5C1.

Rule numbers for notes: 7.7B2, 7.7B4, 7.7B6a, 7.7B6b, 7.7B7, 7.7B7 and 7.7B9 combined, 7.7B10f, 7.7B14, 7.7B17, 7.7B19.

Example 7

```
Type: g      Bib lvl: m Source: d    Lang: eng
Type mat: v Enc lvl: I Govt pub:    Ctry: fr
Int lvl: g  Mod rec:   Tech: l     Leng: 091
Accomp:     MEBE: 0    Dat tp: s   Dates: 1981,
Desc: a
  1   010
  2   040     XXX ‡c XXX
  3   007     v ‡b f ‡d c ‡e b ‡f a ‡h h ‡h o ‡i m
  4   090     PQ2631.O ‡a PN1995.9.F4
  5   092     791.436353
  6   049     XXXX
  7   130 0   Cage aux folles (Motion picture). ‡l English.
  8   245 10  Birds of a feather ‡h videorecording : ‡b a film / ‡c pro-
duced by Marcello Danon ; directed by Edouard Molinaro.
  9   260     [Farmington Hills, MI : ‡b Magnetic Video, ‡c 1981]
 10   300     1 videocassette (91 min.) : ‡b sd., col. ; ‡c 1/2 in.
 11   500     Dubbed into English.
 12   500     Title on container: La cage aux folles = Birds of a
feather.
 13   511 1   Ugo Tognazzi, Michel Serrault, Carmen Scarpitta, Remi
Laurent, Benny Luke, Luisa Maneri, Michel Galabru.
 14   508     Screenplay, Francis Veber, Edouard Molinaro, Marcello
Danon, Jean Poiret ; music, Ennio Morricone ; director of photography,
Armando Nannuzzi.
 15   500     Based on: La cage aux folles / Jean Poiret.
 16   500     A co-production of Les Productions artistes associ´es and
Da Ma produzione SPA, originally produced as French-Italian motion
picture in 1979. Released in the United States by United Artists.
 17   538     VHS.
 18   500     Rating: R.
 19   520     A farce involving a flamboyant homosexual couple's attempt
to appear to be conventional parents in front of the prospective in-laws
of the son of one of the men.
 20   500     "MC: 4506-30."
 21   650 0   Feature films.
 22   700 11  Danon, Marcello.
 23   700 11  Molinaro, Edouard.
 24   700 11  Tognazzi, Ugo.
 25   700 11  Serrault, Michel, ‡d 1928-
 26   700 11  Poiret, Jean, ‡d 1926- ‡t Cage aux folles.
 27   710 21  Productions artistes associ´es.
 28   710 21  Da Ma produzione, S.P.A.
 29   710 21  Magnetic Video.
```

48

Example 8

Title screens

THE NATIONAL FILM BOARD OF CANADA presents

L'OFFICE NATIONAL DU FILM DU CANADA présente
_____

IN PRAISE OF HANDS
a national film board of canada production

HOMMAGE AUX MAINS
production office national du fiom du canada

© NATIONAL FILM BOARD OF CANADA MCMLXXIV
_____

directed by   réalisation
DONALD WINKLER
_____

executive producer   direction génerals
COLIN LOW

This film was produced in co-operation with
the World Crafts Council
and the Sports and Recreation Bureau
of the Province of Ontario.

Ce film a été produit avec la collaboration
de Conseil mondial de l'Artisanat
et la Direction des Sports et Loisirs
du Gouvernement de l'Ontario.

Container label

National Film Board of Canada
Office national du film du Canada

It is illegal to reproduce this film in whole or in part by
videotape, videodisc or any other format whatsoever

All theatrical and television rights reserved

IN PRAISE OF HANDS
HOMMAGE AUX MAINS
106C 0374 109
FOOTAGE 1023' 27 MIN. 35 SEC.

Il est illégal de reproduire ce film en tout ou en partie, au
moyen de ruban magnétoscopique, disque magnétoscopique
ou toute autre forme quelle qu'elle soit.

Tous droits de salles et de télévision reservés.

Example 8

> In praise of hands [motion picture] = Hommage aux mains / directed by
> Donald Winkler ; executive producer, Colin Low ; a National Film
> Board of Canada production. -- [Canada] : National Film Board of
> Canada, c1974.
>   1 film reel (28 min.) : sd., col. ; 16 mm.
>
>   "Produced in co-operation with the World Crafts Council and the
> Sports and Recreation Bureau of the Province of Ontario."
>   Without narration.
>   Summary: Shows people in Japan, Nigeria, Mexico, and Poland as
> they use their hands in creating works of art. Shows the creation
> of pottery, rugs, fabric, sculpture, puppets, and other hand-
> crafted objects.
>
>   1. Decorative arts. 2. Handicraft. I. Winkler, Donald. II.
> Low, Colin. III. National Film Board of Canada. IV. Title:
> Hommage aux mains.

> NK600
> 745.5

This Canadian film has all information given in both languages. We have used the parallel titles, but transcribed only the English information elsewhere. If we were cataloging for a Canadian library, we would want to use most, if not all, of the parallel information.

Rule numbers for notes: 7.7B6, 7.7B10a, 7.7B17.

```
Type: g      Bib lvl: m Source: d   Lang: eng
Type mat: m Enc lvl: I Govt pub: f Ctry: xxc
Int lvl: e  Mod rec:   Tech: l     Leng: 091
Accomp:     MEBE: 0    Dat tp: s   Dates: 1974,
Desc: a
 1    010
 2    040     XXX ǂc XXX
 3    007     m ǂb r ǂd c ǂe a ǂf a ǂg a ǂh d ǂi u
 4    090     NK600
 5    092     745.5 ǂ2 20
 6    049     XXXX
 7    245 00  In praise of hands ǂh motion picture ǂb = Hommage aux mains
ǂc / directed by Donald Winkler ; executive producer, Colin Low ; a
National Film Board of Canada production.
 8    260     [Canada] : ǂb National Film Board of Canada, ǂc c1974.
 9    300     1 film reel (28 min.) : ǂb sd., col. ; ǂc 16 mm.
10    500     "Produced in co-operation with the World Crafts Council and
the Sports and Recreation Bureau of the Province of Ontario."
11    500     Without narration.
12    520     Shows people in Japan, Nigeria, Mexico, and Poland as they
use their hands in creating works of art. Shows the creation of pottery,
rugs, fabric, sculpture, puppets, and other hand-crafted objects.
13    650  0  Decorative arts.
14    650  0  Handicraft.
15    700 11  Winkler, Donald.
16    700 11  Low, Colin.
17    710 21  National Film Board of Canada.
18    740 01  Hommage aux mains.
```

Example 9

Title screens

CBS/Fox Video

Batman

William Dozier Production
starring
Adam West
Burt Ward
and the Rogues Gallery of Villains
The Catwoman
Lee Meriwether
The Joker
Cesar Romero
The Penguin
Burgess Meredith
The Riddler
Frank Gorshin
Music by Nelson Riddle
Written by Lorenzo Semple, Jr.
Produced by
William Dozier
Directed by
Leslie H. Martinson

Example 9

Back of cassette box

Example 9

```
Batman (Motion picture : 1966)
    Batman [videorecording] / Twentieth Century Fox ; produced by
William Dozier ; directed by Leslie H. Martinson ; written by Lorenzo
Semple, Jr. -- [New York] : CBS/Fox Video, [1989]
    1 videocassette (104 min.) : sd., col. ; 1/2 in.

    Closed-captioned for the hearing impaired.
    Title on container: Batman, the movie.
    Cast: Adam West, Burt Ward, Lee Meriwether, Cesar Romero, Burgess
Meredith, Frank Gorshin.
    Music by Nelson Riddle.
    Originally produced as motion picture in 1966; based on the tele-
vision series.
    "Recorded in hi-fi"--Container.
    VHS.
    Summary: Fantastic gadgets abound as Batman and Robin fight a
gallery of villains in order for good to triumph over evil.

    1. Feature films.  2. Films for the hearing impaired.  I. Dozier,
William.  II. Martinson, Leslie H.  III. Semple, Lorenzo.  IV. West,
Adam.  V. Ward, Burt.  VI. Meriwether, Lee, 1935-  VII. Romero,
Cesar, 1907-  VIII. Meredith, Burgess, 1908-  IX. Gorshin, Frank.  X.
Riddle, Nelson.  XI. Twentieth Century-Fox Film Corporation.  XII.
CBS/Fox Video.  XIII. Batman (Television program).  XIV. Title:
Batman, the movie.

PN1995.9.B4
791.436375
```

Examples 9 and 10 show two movies with the same title. A uniform title main entry may be used for each, with qualifiers chosen to distinguish between the two, and to distinguish from the television series, and from the original comic book character. If you have no conflict in your catalog, you can omit the uniform titles.

Rule numbers for notes (Example 9): 7.7B2, 7.7B4, 7.7B6a, 7.7B6b, 7.7B7, 7.7B10a, 7.7B10f, 7.7B17.

Example 9

```
Type: g      Bib lvl: m Source: d    Lang: eng
Type mat: v Enc lvl: I Govt pub:    Ctry: cau
Int lvl: g  Mod rec:   Tech: c      Leng: 104
Accomp:      MEBE: 0    Dat tp: p   Dates: 1989,1966
Desc: a
 1   010
 2   040      XXX ‡c XXX
 3   007      v ‡b f ‡d c ‡e b ‡f a ‡g h ‡h o ‡i s
 4   090      PN1995.9.B4
 5   092      791.436375 ‡2 20
 6   049      XXXX
 7   130 0    Batman (Motion picture : 1966)
 8   245 00   Batman ‡h videorecording / ‡c Twentieth Century Fox ; produced
by William Dozier ; directed by Leslie H. Martinson ; written by Lorenzo
Semple, Jr.
 9   260      [New York] : ‡b CBS/Fox Video, ‡c [1989]
10   300      1 videocassette (104 min.) : ‡b sd., col. ; ‡c 1/2 in.
11   500      Closed-captioned for the hearing impaired.
12   500      Title on container: Batman, the movie.
13   511 1    Adam West, Burt Ward, Lee Meriwether, Cesar Romero, Burgess
Meredith, Frank Gorshin.
14   500      Music by Nelson Riddle.
15   500      Originally produced as motion picture in 1966; based on the
television series.
16   500      "Recorded in hi-fi"--Container.
17   538      VHS.
18   520      Fantastic gadgets abound as Batman and Robin fight a gallery
of villains in order for good to triumph over evil.
19   650 0    Feature films.
20   650 0    Films for the hearing impaired.
21   700 11   Dozier, William.
22   700 11   Martinson, Leslie H.
23   700 11   Semple, Lorenzo.
24   700 11   West, Adam.
25   700 11   Ward, Burt.
26   700 11   Meriwether, Lee, ‡d 1935-
27   700 11   Romero, Cesar, ‡d 1907-
28   700 11   Meredith, Burgess,‡d 1908-
29   700 11   Gorshin, Frank.
30   700 11   Riddle, Nelson.
31   710 21   Twentieth Century-Fox Film Corporation.
32   710 21   CBS/Fox Video.
33   730 01   Batman (Television program)
34   740 01   Batman, the movie.
```

54

Example 10

Title screens

Warner Home Video
———————

Warner Bros. Pictures
Warner Bros.
presents
Jack Nicholson
Michael Keaton
Kim Basinger
A
Guber-Peters Company
production
A Tim Burton Film
BATMAN
Based upon characters appearing
in magazines published by
D.C. Comics, Inc.
Robert Wuhl
Pat Hingle
Billy Dee Williams
Michael Gough
and
Jack Palance
Music by
Danny Elfman
Songs
written and performed by
Prince
based on Batman
characters created by
Bob Kane
Executive Producers
Benjamin Melniker
and
Michael E. Uslan
Co-producer
Chris Kenny
Screenplay by
Sam Hamm
and
Warren Skaaren
Story by
Sam Hamm
Produced by
Jon Peters
and
Peter Guber
Directed by
Tim Burton

Example 10

From the side of the cassette container

```
Batman (Motion picture : 1989)
    Batman [videorecording] / Warner Bros. ; a Guber-Peters Company
production ; a Tim Burton film ; produced by Jon Peters and Peter
Guber ; directed by Tim Burton ; screenplay by Sam Hamm and Warren
Skaaren ; story by Sam Hamm -- [Burbank, CA] : Warner Home Video,
1989.
    1 videocassette (126 min.) : sd., col. ; 1/2 in.

    Closed-captioned for the hearing impaired.
    Cast: Jack Nicholson, Michael Keaton, Kim Basinger, Robert Wuhl,
Pat Hingle, Billy Dee Williams, Michael Gough, Jack Palance.
    Music by Danny Elfman ; songs written and performed by Prince.
    Based on Batman characters created by Bob Kane, published by DC
Comics.
    Originally produced as motion picture in 1989.
    "Digitally processed; Dolby surround stereo; Hi-fi"--Container.
VHS.
    Rated PG-13.
    Summary: A naturalistic treatment of the Batman stories in which
the superhero battles with his arch enemy, The Joker.
    Preceded by Coca-Cola commercial and ad for Warner Bros. merchan-
dise catalog.

    1. Feature films. 2. Films for the hearing impaired.  I. Peters,
Jon.  II. Guber, Peter.  III. Burton, Tim.  IV. Hamm, Sam.  V.
Skaaren, Warren.  VI.  Nicholson, Jack.  VII. Keaton, Michael, 1951-
VIII. Basinger, Kim.  IX. Wuhl, Robert.  X. Hingle, Pat.  XI. Wil-
liams, Billy Dee.  XII. Gough, Michael, 1917-  XIII. Palance, Jack,
1920-  XIV. Elfman, Danny.  XV. Prince.  XVI. Warner Bros.  XVII.
Warner Home Video.

PN1995.9.B4
791.436375
```

This film is preceded by two advertisements.
    Rule numbers for notes (Example 10): 7.7B2, 7.7B6a, 7.7B6b, 7.7B7, 7.7B7, 7.7B10a, 7.7B10f, 7.7B14,
7.7B17, 7.7B18.

Example 10

```
Type: g      Bib lvl: m Source: d   Lang: eng
Type mat: v  Enc lvl: I Govt pub:    Ctry: cau
Int lvl: g   Mod rec:   Tech: l      Leng: 126
Accomp:      MEBE: 0    Dat tp: s    Dates: 1989,
Desc: a
   1  010
   2  040      XXX ǂc XXX
   3  007      v ǂb f ǂd c ǂe b ǂf a ǂg h ǂh o ǂi s
   4  090      PN1995.9.B4
   5  092      791.436375 ǂ2 20
   6  049      XXXX
   7  130 0    Batman (Motion picture : 1989)
   8  245 00   Batman ǂh videorecording / ǂc Warner Bros. ; a Guber-Peters
Company production ; a Tim Burton film ; produced by Jon Peters and
Peter Guber ; directed by Tim Burton ; screenplay by Sam Hamm and Warren
Skaaren ; story by Sam Hamm
   9  260      [Burbank, CA] : ǂb Warner Home Video, ǂc 1989.
  10  300      1 videocassette (126 min.) : ǂb sd., col. ; ǂc 1/2 in.
  11  500      Closed-captioned for the hearing impaired.
  12  511 1    Jack Nicholson, Michael Keaton, Kim Basinger, Robert Wuhl,
Pat Hingle, Billy Dee Williams, Michael Gough, Jack Palance.
  13  500      Music by Danny Elfman ; songs written and performed by
Prince.
  14  500      Based on Batman characters created by Bob Kane, published
by DC Comics.
  15  500      Originally produced as motion picture in 1989.
  16  500      "Digitally processed; Dolby surround stereo; Hi-fi"--Con-
tainer.
  17  538      VHS.
  18  500      Rated PG-13.
  19  520      A naturalistic treatment of the Batman stories in which the
superhero battles with his arch enemy, The Joker.
  20  500      Preceded by Coca-Cola commercial and ad for Warner Bros.
merchandise catalog.
  21  650 0    Feature films.
  22  650 0    Films for the hearing impaired.
  23  700 11   Peters, Jon.
  24  700 11   Guber, Peter.
  25  700 11   Burton, Tim.
  26  700 11   Hamm, Sam.
  27  700 11   Skaaren, Warren.
  28  700 11   Nicholson, Jack.
  29  700 11   Keaton, Michael, ǂd 1951-
  30  700 11   Basinger, Kim.
  31  700 11   Wuhl, Robert.
  32  700 11   Hingle, Pat.
  33  700 11   Williams, Billy Dee.
  34  700 11   Gough, Michael, ǂd 1917-
  35  700 11   Palance, Jack, ǂd 1920-
  36  700 11   Elfman, Danny.
  37  700 01   Prince.
  38  710 21   Warner Bros.
  39  710 21   Warner Home Video.
```

"Dat tp" " p" is not used when the date of production of the movie and date of release in this format are the same.

Example 11

Title screens

Metro-Goldwyn-Mayer
presents
The Wizard
of Oz
A
Victor Fleming
Production
Judy Garland
Frank Morgan
Ray Bolger
Bert Lahr
Jack Haley
Billie Burke
Margaret Hamilton
Charley Grapewin
and **The Munchkins**
Screen play by
Noel Langley,
Florence Ryerson,
and Edgar Allan Woolf
Adaptation by
Noel Langley
From the book by
L. Frank Baum
Musical Adaptation by
Herbert Stothart
Lyrics by
E. Y. Harburg
Music by
Harold Arlen
Produced by
Mervyn LeRoy
Directed by
Victor Fleming

Example 11A
The 1980 videocassette

```
Wizard of Oz (Motion picture)
    The Wizard of Oz [videorecording] / Metro-Goldwyn-Mayer ; produced
by Mervyn LeRoy ; directed by Victor Fleming ; screen play by Noel
Langley, Florence Ryerson, and Edgar Allan Woolf ; adaptation by Noel
Langley. -- [New York, N.Y : CBS Video, 1980]
    1 videocassette (101 min.) : sd., col. with b&w opening and clos-
ing sequences ; 1/2 in.

    Cast: Judy Garland (Dorothy), Frank Morgan (Provessor Marvel;
Wizard of Oz), Ray Bolger (Hunk; Scarecrow), Bert Lahr (Zeke; Cow-
ardly Lion), Jack Haley (Hickory; Tin Man), Billie Burke (Glinda),
Margaret Hamilton (Mrs. Gulch; Wicked Witch of the West), Charley
Grapewin (Uncle Henry), the Munchkins.
    Musical adaptation by Herbert Stothart ; music by Harold Arlen ;
lyrics by E.Y. Harburg.
    Originally produced as motion picture in 1939.
    "From the book by L. Frank Baum."
    VHS.
    Summary: Dorothy, her dog Toto, and three friends set off for the
mysterious Emerald City in search of the Wizard. Although pursued by
the Wicked Witch of the West, they reach the Emerald City and receive
an audience with the Wizard.

    1. Feature films.  2. Fantastic films.  I. LeRoy, Mervyn, 1900-
1987.  II. Fleming, Victor, 1883-1949.  III. Langley, Noel, 1911-
IV. Ryerson, Florence, 1894-  V. Woolf, Edgar Allan.  VI. Garland,
Judy.  VII. Morgan, Frank, 1890-1949.  VIII. Bolger, Ray.  IX. Lahr,
Bert, 1895-1967.  X. Haley, Jack, 1899-1979.  XI. Burke, Billie,
1885-1970.  XII. Hamilton, Margaret, 1902-  XIII. Grapewin, Charley,
1869-1956.  XIV. Stothart, Herbert, 1885-1949.  XV. Arlen, Harold,
1905-1986.  XVI  Harburg, E. Y., 1905-1981.  XVII. Baum, L. Frank
(Lyman Frank), 1865-1919.  Wizard of Oz.  XVIII. Metro-Goldwyn-Mayer.
XIX. CBS Video.

PN1995.9.F36 (fantastic film)
PS3503.A923W (Baum's number)
791.436372
```

Rule numbers for notes: 7.7B6a, 7.7B6b, 7.7B7, 7.7B7, 7.7B10f, 7.7B17.

Example 11B
The 50th anniversary videodisc

Label of videodisc

```
Wizard of Oz (Motion picture : 50th anniversary limited ed.)
    The Wizard of Oz [videorecording] / Metro-Goldwyn-Mayer ; produced
by Mervyn LeRoy ; directed by Victor Fleming ; screen play by Noel
Langley, Florence Ryerson, and Edgar Allan Woolf ; adaptation by Noel
Langley. -- 50th anniversary limited ed. -- [Culver City, CA] : MGM/
UA Home Video, [1989]
    1 videodisc (119 min.) : sd., col. with b&w opening and closing
sequences ; 12 in. + 1 booklet (32 p. : ill. ; 22 cm.)

    Closed-captioned for the hearing impaired.
    Cast: Judy Garland (Dorothy), Frank Morgan (Professor Marvel;
Wizard of Oz), Ray Bolger (Hunk; Scarecrow), Bert Lahr (Zeke; Cow-
ardly Lion), Jack Haley (Hickory; Tin Man), Billie Burke (Glinda)
Margaret Hamilton (Mrs. Gulch; Wicked Witch of the West), Charley
Grapewin (Uncle Henry), the Munchkins.
    Musical adaptation by Herbert Stothart ; music by Harold Arlen ;
lyrics by E.Y. Harburg.
    Originally produced as motion picture in 1939.
    "From the book by L. Frank Baum."
    Opening and closing sequences restored to the orginal sepia.
    "LaserVision; extended play; digital sound; chapter search"--
Container.
    Booklet describes and illustrates the film production.
    Issued also as VHS videocassette.
    Summary: Dorothy, her dog Toto, and three friends set off for the
mysterious Emerald City in search of the Wizard. Although pursued by
```
(continued on next page)

the Wicked Witch of the West, they reach the Emerald City and receive an audience with the Wizard.

Includes footage cut from the original release, dress rehearsal film, and the first soundtrack recording of If I only had a heart, sung by Buddy Ebsen, the original Tin Man.

1. Feature films. 2. Fantastic films. 3. Films for the hearing impaired. I. LeRoy, Mervyn, 1900-1987. II. Fleming, Victor, 1883-1949. III. Langley, Noel, 1911- IV. Ryerson, Florence, 1894- V. Woolf, Edgar Allan. VI. Garland, Judy. VII. Morgan, Frank, 1890-1949. VIII. Bolger, Ray. IX. Lahr, Bert, 1895-1967. X. Haley, Jack, 1899-1979. XI. Burke, Billie, 1885-1970. XII. Hamilton, Margaret, 1902- XIII. Grapewin, Charley, 1869-1956. XIV. Stothart, Herbert, 1885-1949. XV. Arlen, Harold, 1905-1986. XVI. Harburg, E. Y., 1905-1981. XVII. Ebsen, Buddy. XVIII. Baum, L. Frank (Lyman Frank), 1865-1919. Wizard of Oz. XIX. Metro-Goldwyn-Mayer. XX. MGM/UA Home Video.

PN1995.9.F36 (fantastic film)
PS3503.A923W (Baum's number)
731.436372

Title and credits screens are the same for each of this pair of examples. The first is the 1980 VHS videocassette. The second is the 1989 50th anniversary videodisc. The 50th anniversary edition, available in VHS and laserdisc, includes additional material as listed in the last note. A booklet about the production accompanies the disc. The opening and closing sequences, black-and-white in the 1980 release, have been restored to their original sepia coloring. The rules instruct us to record sepia as b&w in the physical description, but I made a note about it as this restoration is important.

A uniform title main entry is needed to distinguish between the two editions, if you have both in your catalog.

Rule numbers for notes: 7.7B2, 7.7B6a, 7.7B6b, 7.7B7, 7.7B7, 7.7B10c, 7.7B10f, 7.7B11, 7.7B16, 7.7B17, 7.7B18.

Example 11B
The 50th anniversary videodisc

```
Type: g       Bib lvl: m Source: d    Lang: eng
Type mat: v Enc lvl: I Govt pub:      Ctry: cau
Int lvl: g  Mod rec:   Tech: l        Leng: 119
Accomp:     MEBE: 0    Dat tp: s      Dates: 1989,
Desc: a
 1   010
 2   040     XXX ǂc XXX
 3   007     v ǂb d ǂd m ǂe g ǂf a ǂg h ǂh z ǂi s
 4   090     PN1995.9.F36 ǂa PS3503.A923W
 5   092     791.436372 ǂ2 20
 6   049     XXXX
 7   130 0   Wizard of Oz (Motion picture : 50th anniversary limited
ed.)
 8   245 04  The Wizard of Oz ǂh videorecording / ǂc Metro-Goldwyn-Mayer
; produced by Mervyn LeRoy ; directed by Victor Fleming ; screen play by
Noel Langley, Florence Ryerson, and Edgar Allan Woolf ; adaptation by
Noel Langley.
```

(continued on next page)

```
 9   250        50th anniversary limited ed.
10   260        [Culver City, CA] : ǂb MGM/UA Home Video, ǂc [1989]
11   300        1 videodisc (119 min.) : ǂb sd., col. with b&w opening and
closing sequences ; ǂc 12 in. + ǂe 1 booklet (32 p. : ill. ; 22 cm.)
12   500        Closed-captioned for the hearing impaired.
13   511 1      Judy Garland (Dorothy), Frank Morgan (Professor Marvel;
Wizard of Oz), Ray Bolger (Hunk; Scarecrow), Bert Lahr (Zeke; Cowardly
Lion), Jack Haley (Hickory; Tin Man), Billie Burke (Glinda) Margaret
Hamilton (Mrs. Gulch; Wicked Witch of the West), Charley Grapewin (Uncle
Henry), the Munchkins.
14   500        Musical adaptation by Herbert Stothart ; music by Harold
Arlen ; lyrics by E.Y. Harburg.
15   500        Originally produced as motion picture in 1939.
16   500        "From the book by L. Frank Baum."
17   500        Opening and closing sequences restored to the orginal se-
pia.
18   500        "LaserVision; extended play; digital sound; chapter
search"--Container.
19   500        Booklet describes and illustrates the film production.
20   500        Issued also as VHS videocassette.
21   520        Dorothy, her dog Toto, and three friends set off for the
mysterious Emerald City in search of the Wizard. Although pursued by the
Wicked Witch of the West, they reach the Emerald City and receive an
audience with the Wizard.
22   500        Includes footage cut from the original release, dress re-
hearsal film, and the first soundtrack recording of If I only had a
heart, sung by Buddy Ebsen, the original Tin Man.
23   650 0      Feature films.
24   650 0      Fantastic films.
25   650 0      Films for the hearing impaired.
26   700 11     LeRoy, Mervyn, $d 1900-1987.
27   700 11     Fleming, Victor, $d 1883-1949.
28   700 11     Langley, Noel, $d 1911-
29   700 11     Ryerson, Florence, $d 1894-
30   700 11     Woolf, Edgar Allan.
31   700 11     Garland, Judy.
32   700 11     Morgan, Frank, ǂd 1890-1949.
33   700 11     Bolger, Ray.
34   700 11     Lahr, Bert, ǂd 1895-1967.
35   700 11     Haley, Jack, ǂd 1899-1979.
36   700 11     Burke, Billie, ǂd 1885-1970.
37   700 11     Hamilton, Margaret, ǂd 1902-
38   700 11     Grapewin, Charley, ǂd 1869-1956.
39   700 11     Stothart, Herbert, ǂd 1885-1949.
40   700 11     Arlen, Harold, ǂd 1905-1986.
41   700 11     Harburg, E. Y., 1905-1981.
42   700 11     Ebsen, Buddy.
43   700 11     Baum, L. Frank (Lyman Frank), ǂd 1865-1919. ǂt Wizard of
Oz.
44   710 21     Metro-Goldwyn-Mayer.
45   710 21     MGM/UA Home Video.
```

"Date tp" is coded "s" in this example because it is a new work, including additional material.

Example 12

Title screens

MGM/UA Home Video

A Selznick International Picture
Selznick International
in association with
Metro-Goldwyn-Mayer
has the honor to present its
Technicolor production of
Margaret Mitchell's
Story of the Old South

Gone With The Wind

starring
Clark Gable as *Rhett Butler*
Vivien Leigh as *Scarlett O'Hara*
Leslie Howard as *Ashley Wilkes*
Olivia de Havilland as *Melanie Hamilton*
Produced by David O. Selznick
Screen Play by Sidney Howard
Musical Score by Max Steiner
Directed by Victor Fleming

Label of cassette

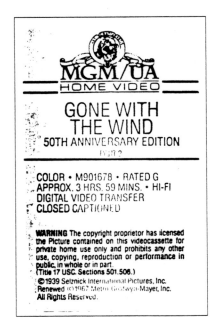

Example 12

    Gone with the wind (Motion picture : 50th anniversary ed.)
    Gone with the wind [videorecording] / Selznick International in
association with Metro-Goldwyn-Mayer ; produced by David O. Selznick
; directed by Victor Fleming ; screen play by Sidney Howard. -- 50th
anniversary ed. -- [Culver City, CA] : MGM/UA Home Video, [1989]
    2 videocassetes (ca. 3 hrs., 59 min.) : sd., col. ; 1/2 in. + 1
booklet ([5] p. : col. ill. ; 22 cm.) in container 23 x 27 x 4 cm.

    Closed-captioned for the hearing impaired.
    Cast: Clark Gable, Vivien Leigh, Leslie Howard, Olivia De
Havilland.
    "Musical score by Max Steiner."
    Based on the novel by Margaret Mitchell.
    Originally produced as motion picture in 1939.
    "Videophonic sound, digitally enhanced for stereo; Dolby system"--
Container.
    VHS.
    Rated G.
    Issued also on videodisc.
    Summary: A fictitious Civil War drama concerning the life of
Scarlett O'Hara (Vivien Leigh), daughter of Gerald O'Hara (Thomas
Mitchell), owner of the southern plantation of Tara, and her amourous
adventures centered around Rhett Butler (Clark Gable), a gambler from
South Carolina, and Ashley Wilkes (Leslie Howard), a southern aristo-
crat and plantation owner from Georgia. Vividly portrays the pre-war
attitudes of southern plantation owners' political views on the
issues of slavery and secession of the South from the Union. Shows
the struggles and final degradation of the southern plantation owners
caused by their defeat in the Civil War and shows, through Scarlett,
the reconstruction trials and tribulations encountered by former
southern belles--who have lost their men folk during the war--to
rebuild the post-Civil War South. Includes a portrayal of the burning of Atlanta by Union troops.
    Feature is followed by highlights from the documentary, The making
of a legend.

    1. Feature films. 2. United States--History--Civil War, 1861-
1865--Drama. 3. Films for the hearing impaired. I. Selznick, David
O., 1902-1965. II. Fleming, Victor, 1883-1949. III. Howard, Sidney,
1891-1939. IV. Gable, Clark, 1901-1960. V. Leigh, Vivien, 1913-
1967. VI. Howard, Leslie, 1893-1943. VII. De Havilland, Olivia.
VIII. Steiner, Max, 1888-1971. IX. Mitchell, Margaret, 1900-1949.
Gone with the wind. X. Selznick International Pictures. XI. Metro-
Goldwyn-Mayer. XII. MGM/UA Home Video. XIII. Making of a legend
(Television program). Selections. 1989.

PS3523.I972 (number for Margaret Mitchell)
E605 (Civil War)
791.436358

Example 12

Rule numbers for notes: 7.7B2, 7.7B6a, 7.7B6b, 7.7B7, 7.7B7, 7.7B10a, 7.7B10f, 7.7B14, 7.7B16, 7.7B17, 7.7B18.

This film has a uniform title main entry that includes the edition statement. The uniform title is needed for an added entry in the next example.

A uniform title added entry is made for the film cataloged in the next example, because excerpts from it are on this disc.

The date of 1989 does not appear anywhere on the item or its container, but is assumed from the "50th" information.

The series information is not bracketed because it appears on the cassette label.

```
Type: g      Bib lvl: m Source: d    Lang: eng
Type mat: v Enc lvl: I Govt pub:     Ctry: cau
Int lvl: g  Mod rec:   Tech: l       Leng: 231
Accomp:     MEBE: 0    Dat tp: s     Dates: 1989,
Desc: a
   1   010
   2   040      XXX ‡c XXX
   3   007      v ‡b ‡d c ‡e b ‡f a ‡g h ‡h o ‡i s
   4   090      PS3523.I972 ‡a E605
   5   092      791.436358 ‡2 20
   6   049      XXXX
   7   130      Gone with the wind (Motion picture : 50th anniversary ed.)
   8   245 00 Gone with the wind ‡h videorecording / ‡c Selznick Interna-
tional in association with Metro-Goldwyn-Mayer ; produced by David O.
Selznick ; directed by Victor Fleming ; screen play by Sidney Howard.
   9   250      50th anniversary ed.
  10   260      [Culver City, CA] : ‡b MGM/UA Home Video, ‡c [1989]
  11   300      2 videocassetes (ca. 3 hrs., 59 min.) : ‡b sd., col. ; ‡c
1/2 in. + ‡e 1 booklet ([5] p. : col. ill. ; 22 cm.) in container 23 x
27 x 4 cm.
  12   500      Closed-captioned for the hearing impaired.
  13   511 1   Clark Gable, Vivien Leigh, Leslie Howard, Olivia De
Havilland.
  14   500      "Musical score by Max Steiner."
  15   500      Based on the novel by Margaret Mitchell.
  16   500      Originally produced as motion picture in 1939.
  17   500      "Videophonic sound, digitally enhanced for stereo; Dolby
system"--Container.
  18   538      VHS.
  19   500      Rated G.
  20   500      Issued also on videodisc.
  21   520      A fictitious Civil War drama concerning the life of
Scarlett O'Hara (Vivien Leigh), daughter of Gerald O'Hara (Thomas
Mitchell), owner of the southern plantation of Tara, and her amourous
adventures centered around Rhett Butler (Clark Gable), a gambler from
South Carolina, and Ashley Wilkes (Leslie Howard), a southern aristocrat
and plantation owner from Georgia. Vividly portrays the pre-war atti-
tudes of southern plantation owners' political views on the issues of
slavery and secession of the South from the Union.  Shows the struggles
and final degradation of the southern plantation owners caused by their
```

(continued on next page)

defeat in the Civil War and shows, through Scarlett, the reconstruction trials and tribulations encountered by former southern belles--who have lost their men folk during the war--to rebuild the post-Civil War South. Includes a portrayal of the burning of Atlanta by Union troops.

22   500   Feature is followed by highlights from the documentary, The making of a legend.

23   650   0 Feature films.

24   650   0 Video recordings for the hearing impaired.

25   651   0 United States ‡x History ‡y Civil War, 1861-1865 ‡x Drama.

26   700 11 Selznick, David O., ‡d 1902-1965.

27   700 11 Fleming, Victor, ‡d 1883-1949.

28   700 11 Howard, Sidney, ‡d 1891-1939.

29   700 11 Gable, Clark, ‡d 1901-1960.

30   700 11 Leigh, Vivien, ‡d 1913-1967.

31   700 11 Howard, Leslie, ‡d 1893-1943.

32   700 11 De Havilland, Olivia.

33   700 11 Steiner, Max, ‡d 1888-1971.

34   700 11 Mitchell, Margaret, ‡d 1900-1949. ‡t Gone with the wind.

35   710 21 Selznick International Pictures.

36   710 21 Metro-Goldwyn-Mayer.

37   710 21 MGM/UA Home Video.

38   730 01 Making of a legend (Television program). ‡k Selections. ‡f 1989.

66

Example 13

Title screens

MGM/UA Home Video
————————

A Turner Entertainment Presentation in association with
Selznick Properties LTD
The Making of a Legend
Gone with the Wind
Narrated by **Christopher Plummer**
Executive Producers
Daniel Mayer Selznick
L. Jeffrey Selznick
Written by David Thomson
Produced by L. Jeffrey Selznick
Directed by David Hinton

Back of
cassette container

Example 13

```
Making of a legend (Television program)
   The making of a legend [videorecording] : Gone with the wind /
executive producers, Daniel Mayer Selznick, L. Jeffrey Selznick ;
produced by L. Jeffrey Selznick ; directed by David Hinton. ; written
by David Thomson -- [Culver City, Calif.] : MGM/UA Home Video,
[1989], c1988.
   1 videocassette (ca. 124 min.) : sd., col. with b&w sequences ;
1/2 in.

   Documentary, produced for television, about making the movie Gone
with the wind.
   Narrator: Christopher Plummer.
   "A Turner Entertainment presentation in association with Selznick
Properties, Ltd."
   VHS.

   1. Gone with the wind (Motion picture)  2.  Motion pictures--
Production and direction.  I. Selznick, Daniel Mayer.  II. Selznick,
L. Jeffrey.  III. Hinton, David B., 1950-  IV. Thomson, David, 1941-
V. Plummer, Christopher.  VI. Turner Entertainment Co.  VII. Selznick
Properties, Ltd.  VIII. MGM/UA Home Video.  IX. Gone with the wind
(Motion picture).  Selections.  1989.

PN1994
791.43
```

This documentary needs a subject heading for *Gone with the wind* because it is about the production of the film. It also needs an added entry for the film because it includes scenes from the film. Note the qualifier on the uniform title used as subject and added entry. It uses the wording of the GMD, but is capitalized rather than entirely lower case, and it is in parentheses rather than brackets. The uniform title main entry here is based on the uniform title added entry needed for the previous example. According to *AACR 2* rule 25.2C1, the initial article is omitted.

The place of publication included the full name of the state. It is abbreviated as shown. The postal abbreviation may be used only if found on the item.

Rule numbers for notes: 7.7B1, 7.7B6a, 7.7B6b.

Copyright date given on the video is 1988. On the container, 1989 is given as the copyright for the package design, so it is used as date of publication.

Example 13

```
Type: g       Bib lvl: m Source: d    Lang: eng
Type mat: v Enc lvl: I Govt pub:      Ctry: cau
Int lvl: e  Mod rec:   Tech: l        Leng: 124
Accomp:     MEBE: 0    Dat tp: p    Dates: 1989,1988
Desc: a
 1    010
 2    040       XXX ǂc XXX
 3    007       v ǂb f ǂd m ǂe b ǂf a ǂg h ǂh o ǂi s
 4    090       PN1994
 5    092       791.43 ǂ2 20
 6    049       XXXX
 7    130 0  Making of a legend (Television program)
 8    245 04  The making of a legend ǂh videorecording : ǂb Gone with the
wind / ǂc executive producers, Daniel Mayer Selznick, L. Jeffrey
Selznick ; produced by L. Jeffrey Selznick ; directed by David Hinton. ;
written by David Thomson
 9    260       [Culver City, Calif.] : ǂb MGM/UA Home Video, ǂc [1989],
c1988.
10    300       1 videocassette (ca. 124 min.) : ǂb sd., col. with b&w
sequences ; ǂc 1/2 in.
11    500       Documentary, produced for television, about making the
movie Gone with the wind.
12    511 3  Christopher Plummer.
13    500       "A Turner Entertainment presentation in association with
Selznick Properties, Ltd."
14    538       VHS.
15    630 00  Gone with the wind (Motion picture)
16    650  0  Motion pictures ǂx Production and direction.
17    700 11  Selznick, Daniel Mayer.
18    700 11  Selznick, L. Jeffrey.
19    700 11  Hinton, David B., ǂd 1950-
20    700 11  Thomson, David, ǂd 1941-
21    700 11  Plummer, Christopher.
22    710 21  Turner Entertainment Co.
23    710 21  Selznick Properties, Ltd.
24    710 21  MGM/UA Home Video.
25    730 01  Gone with the wind (Motion picture). ǂk Selections. ǂf
1989.
```

"Date tp" "p" is used for this item copyrighted in 1988 and distributed the following year.

Example 14

Title screens

CMV
Enterprises
Michael Jackson
MOONWALKER

— — — — —

[at end: ca. 5 min. of credits]
Smooth Criminal
directed by Colin Chilvers
produced by
Dennis E. Jones
Screenplay by David Newman
based on a story by
Michael Jackson

— — — — —

Executive producers
Michael Jackson
Frank Dileo
Original music by
Peter Broughton

— — — — —

Anthology segments
directed by
Jerry Kramer
produced by
Jerry Kramer

From side of cassette container

Example 14

```
Jackson, Michael, 1958-
    Moonwalker [videorecording] / CMV Enterprises ; Michael Jackson.
-- [New York, NY : CBS Music Video Enterprises], c1988.
    1 videocassette (94 min.) : sd., col. ; 1/2 in.

    Anthology of film segments starring Michael Jackson.
    Smooth criminal directed by Colin Chilvers ; produced by Dennis E.
Jones ; screenplay by David Newman, based on a story by Michael
Jackson ; original music by Bruce Broughton.
    Anthology segments produced, directed by Jerry Kramer.
    "Digital audio, Dolby system, on linear tracks"--Container.
    VHS hi-fi stereo.
    Preceded by Pepsi commercial: I'm bad.
    Contents: Man in the mirror [live performance] -- Retrospective of
24 years of hits -- Badder [I'm bad, done with child performers] --
Speed demon [chase scene using Claymation] -- Leave me alone [com-
ments on media attention, using live action and animation] -- Smooth
criminal [A superhero (Michael) pits himself and all his powers
against the evil Mr. Big (Joe Pesci) who is attempting to take over
the world by getting kids hooked on drugs](ca. 40 min.) -- Come
together [live performance] -- The moon is walking (performed by
Ladysmith Black Mombazo).

    1. Popular music--United States.  2. Music videos.  I. Jones,
Dennis E.  II. Newman, David.  III. Broughton, Bruce, 1945-  IV.
Kramer, Jerry, 1936-  V. Pesci, Joe.  VI. CBS Music Video Enter-
prises.  VII. Ladysmith Black Mombazo.  VIII. CMV Enterprises.  IX.
Title: I'm bad.  X. Title: Man in the mirror.  XI. Title: Badder.
XII. Title: Come together. XIII. Title: Smooth criminal.  XIV. Title:
The moon is walking.

    M1630.18
    781.63
```

This music video has more credits than anything I've ever seen. I attempted to extract the most important credits for the cataloging, but I could not read the credits for composer, etc., for the music in each segment. An LCRI for 7.1F1 (*CSB* 36) permits us to use the name of the star of a music video in the statement of responsibility. As principal performer, he is also chosen as main entry. This is permitted by the rule interpretation for 21.23 (*CSB* 45).

The contents note combines contents and summary information, with some cast and credits information as well. The summary information is bracketed in, as it is not taken directly from the source of the contents.

If the contents were straight song titles, we would make analytical added entries for all. As they are different types of material, the songs and the story were selected for added entries. Composer-uniform title added entries should be used for the songs, but I couldn't read the composer information in the credits, and I couldn't find the information in OCLC, so I've made added entires for the titles as they appear on the item.

Rule numbers for notes: 7.7B1 combined with 7.7B6a, 7.7B6b, 7.7B7, 7.7B10a, 7.7B10 a and f, 7.7B18 combined with 7.7B17.

There is a period after the closing parenthesis in the contents note. In the notes, a bracket or parenthesis is not considered closing punctuation, according to LCRI 1.7A1 (*CSB* 44), so a period must be added.

Example 14

```
Type: g      Bib lvl: m Source: d    Lang: eng
Type mat: v  Enc lvl: I Govt pub:    Ctry: xxu
Int lvl: g   Mod rec:   Tech: l      Leng: 094
Accomp:      MEBE: 0    Dat tp: s    Dates: 1988
Desc: a
  1   010
  2   040      XXX ‡c XXX
  3   007      v ‡b f ‡d c ‡e b ‡f a ‡g h ‡h o ‡i s
  4   090      M1630.18
  5   092      781.63
  6   049      XXXX
  7   100 1    Jackson, Michael, ‡d 1958-
  8   245 10   Moonwalker ‡h videorecording / ‡c CMV Enterprises ; Michael
Jackson.
  9   260      [New York, NY : ‡b CBS Music Video Enterprises], ‡c c1988.
 10   300      1 videocassette (94 min.) : ‡b sd., col. ; ‡c 1/2 in.
 11   500      Anthology of film segments starring Michael Jackson.
 12   500      Smooth criminal directed by Colin Chilvers ; produced by
Dennis E. Jones ; screenplay by David Newman, based on a story by
Michael Jackson ; original music by Bruce Broughton.
 13   500      Anthology segments produced, directed by Jerry Kramer.
 14   500      "Digital audio, Dolby system, on linear tracks"--Container.
 15   538      VHS hi-fi stereo.
 16   500      Preceded by Pepsi commercial: I'm bad.
 17   505 0    Man in the mirror [live performance] -- Retrospective of 24
years of hits -- Badder [I'm bad, done with child performers] -- Speed
demon [chase scene using Claymation] -- Leave me alone [comments on
media attention, using live action and animation] -- Smooth criminal [A
superhero (Michael) pits himself and all his powers against the evil Mr.
Big (Joe Pesci) who is attempting to take over the world by getting kids
hooked on drugs](ca. 40 min.) -- Come together [live performance] -- The
moon is walking (performed by Ladysmith Black Mombazo).
 18   650 0    Popular music ‡z United States.
 19   650 0    Music videos.
 20   700 11   Jones, Dennis E.
 21   700 11   Newman, David.
 22   700 11   Broughton, Bruce, ‡d 1945-
 23   700 11   Kramer, Jerry, ‡d 1936-
 24   700 11   Pesci, Joe.
 25   710 21   CBS Music Video Enterprises.
 26   710 21   Ladysmith Black Mombazo.
 27   710 21   CMV Enterprises.
 28   740 01   I'm bad.
 29   740 01   Man in the mirror.
 30   740 01   Badder.
 31   740 01   Come together.
 32   740 01   Smooth criminal.
 33   740 41   The moon is walking.
```

Example 15

Label on videocassette

DEWEY DECIMAL
AND THE
LIBRARIANS

THE VIDEO

No title or credits frames on the video.

```
Dewey Decimal and the Librarians (Musical group)
   Dewey Decimal and the Librarians [videorecording] : the video. --
[Minneapolis? Minn. : s.n., 1989]
   1 videocassette (90 min.) : sd., col. with b&w sequences ; 1/2 in.

   Recording of the performance of Dewey Decimal and the Librarians
at the Macalester College Class of 1964 25 year reunion, June 11,
1989, including the opening slide show.
   Title from cassette label.
   Produced by Robert Stimson.
   VHS.

   1. Folk music--United States.  2. Music videos.  3. Macalester
College.  Class of 1964.  I. Stimson, Robert, 1942-  II. Macalester
College.  Class of 1964.  Reunion (25th : 1989 : Saint Paul, Minn.)

M1629
781.62
```

Although this looks like it might be an unpublished item, it was produced in multiple copies for distribution. It has a corporate main entry for the performing group. The qualifier "musical group" is needed for this name, as the name by itself does not sound like a performing group.
Rule numbers for notes: 7.7B1, 7.7B3, 7.7B6, 7.7B10f.

Example 15

```
Type: g      Bib lvl: m Source: d    Lang: eng
Type mat: v Enc lvl: I Govt pub:    Ctry: mnu
Int lvl: g  Mod rec:   Tech: l      Leng: 090
Accomp:     MEBE: 0    Dat tp: s    Dates: 1989,
Desc: a
 1   010
 2   040     XXX ǂc XXX
 3   007     v ǂb f ǂd m ǂe b ǂf a ǂg h ǂh o ǂi u
 4   090     M1629
 5   092     781.62 ǂ2 20
 6   049     XXXX
 7   110 2   Dewey Decimal and the Librarians (Musical group)
 8   245 10  Dewey Decimal and the Librarians ǂh videorecording : ǂb the
video.
 9   260     [Minneapolis? Minn. : ǂb s.n., ǂc 1989]
10   300     1 videocassette (90 min.) : ǂb sd., col. with b&w sequences
; ǂc 1/2 in.
11   500     Recording of the performance of Dewey Decimal and the Li-
brarians at the Macalester College Class of 1964 25 year reunion, June
11, 1989, including the opening slide show.
12   500     Title from cassette label.
13   500     Produced by Robert Stimson.
14   538     VHS.
15   650 0   Folk music ǂz United States.
16   650 0   Music videos.
17   610 20  Macalester College. ǂb Class of 1964.
18   700 11  Stimson, Robert, ǂd 1942-
19   710 21  Macalester College. ǂb Class of 1964. ǂb Reunion ǂn (25th :
ǂd 1989 : ǂc Saint Paul, Minn.)
```

74

Example 16

Title screens

Live from the Met

Bel Canto
Paramount Home Video

Hansel & Gretel

From the back of the container

This presentation of *Hansel and Gretel* is sung in English and was taped
during the December 25, 1982 performance at the Metropolitan Opera.
No material was taken from rehearsals, other performances
or remake recording sessions.

Metropolitan Opera performances
are also available on Pioneer Artists LaserDisc.™

Bel Canto

PARAMOUNT HOME VIDEO
A Subsidiary of Paramount Pictures Corporation

Example 16

```
Hansel & Gretel [videorecording] / the Metropolitan Opera ; [music
    by Engelbert Humperdinck ; libretto by Adelheid Wette]. -- [Holly-
    wood, CA] : Paramount Home Video, [1987]
        1 videocassette (104 min.) : sd., col. ; 1/2 in. + 1 booklet (8
    p. ; 22 cm.). -- (Bel Canto)

        Opera.
        At head of title: Live from the Met.
        Cast: Judith Blegen (Gretel), Frederica von Stade (Hansel),
    Jean Kraft (Gertrude), Michael Devlin (Peter), Diane Kesling
    (Sandman), Betsy Norden (Dewfairy), Rosalind Elias (Witch) ;
    Metropolitan Opera Orchestra, Metropolitan Opera Chorus, Thomas
    Fulton, conductor.
        Recorded at a telecast performance of the Metropolitan Opera,
    December 25, 1982.
        VHS.
        Booklet includes program notes and synopsis.
        Issued also on laserdisc.

        1. Operas.  I. Blegen, Judith.  II. Von Stade, Frederica.  III.
    Kraft, Jean.  IV. Devlin, Michael.  V. Kesling, Diane.  VI.
    Norden, Betsy.  VII. Elias, Rosalind.  VIII. Fulton, Thomas.  IX.
    Humperdinck, Engelbert, 1854-1921. Hänsel und Gretel.  X. Wette,
    Adelheid, 1858-1916. Hänsel und Gretel.  XI. Metropolitan Opera
    (New York, N.Y.)  XII. Paramount Home Video.  XIII. Title: Hansel
    and Gretel.

M1503.H926H
782.1
```

A Music Cataloging Decision at the Library of Congress (6.7B6, *MCB* vol. 20, no. 6) instructs us on punctuation for performer notes. The semicolon is to be set off by spaces both before and after it. The pattern for orchestra and conductor is to be

  Bergen Symphony Orchestra, Karsten Andersen, conductor.

 This opera video is not entered under the composer, because many creative and production activities are involved in addition to that of composing the music. An entire production of the opera is involved. As responsibility for that total production is diffuse, main entry would be under title.

 Rule numbers for notes: 7.7B1, 7.7B5, 7.7B6a, 7.7B7, 7.7B10f, 7.7B11, 7.7B14.

 I didn't know what to do with the phrase "Bel Canto." It is not in the online authority file through OCLC. I guessed it might be a series.

Example 16

```
Type: g      Bib lvl: m Source: d    Lang: eng
Type mat: v  Enc lvl: I Govt pub:    Ctry: nyu
Int lvl: g   Mod rec:   Tech: 1      Leng: 104
Accomp:      MEBE: 0    Dat tp: s    Dates: 1987
Desc: a
  1    010
  2    040      XXX ‡c XXX
  3    007      v ‡b f ‡d c ‡e b ‡f a ‡g h ‡h o ‡i s
  4    090      M1503.H926 ‡b H
  5    092      782.1 ‡2 20
  6    049      XXXX
  7    245 00   Hansel & Gretel ‡h videorecording / ‡c the Metropolitan
Opera ; [music by Engelbert Humperdinck ; libretto by Adelheid Wette].
  8    260      [Hollywood, CA] : ‡b Paramount Home Video, ‡c [1987]
  9    300      1 videocassette (104 min.) : ‡b sd., col. ; ‡c 1/2 in. + ‡e
1 booklet (8 p. ; 22 cm.)
 10    490  0   Bel Canto.
 11    500      Opera.
 12    500      At head of title: Live from the Met.
 13    511 1    Judith Blegen (Gretel), Frederica von Stade (Hansel), Jean
Kraft (Gertrude), Michael Devlin (Peter), Diane Kesling (Sandman),
Betsy Norden (Dewfairy), Rosalind Elias (Witch) ; Metropolitan Opera
Orchestra, Metropolitan Opera Chorus, Thomas Fulton, conductor.
 14    500      Recorded at a telecast performance of the Metropolitan
Opera, December 25, 1982.
 15    538      VHS.
 16    500      Booklet includes program notes and synopsis.
 17    500      Issued also on laserdisc.
 18    650  0   Operas.
 19    700 11   Blegen, Judith.
 20    700 11   Von Stade, Frederica.
 21    700 11   Kraft, Jean.
 22    700 11   Devlin, Michael.
 23    700 11   Kesling, Diane.
 24    700 11   Norden, Betsy.
 25    700 11   Elias, Rosalind.
 26    700 11   Fulton, Thomas.
 27    700 11   Humperdinck, Engelbert, ‡d 1854-1921. ‡t H¨ansel und
Gretel.
 28    700 11   Wette, Adelheid, ‡d 1858-1916. ‡t H¨ansel und Gretel.
 29    710 21   Metropolitan Opera (New York, N.Y.)
 30    710 21   Paramount Home Video.
 31    740 01   Hansel and Gretel.
```

Example 17

Title screens

Walt Disney Home Video

Walt Disney Classics
Walt Disney Pictures
Walt Disney Presents
Cinderella
from the original classic by
Charles Perrault
Color by Technicolor
Directors
Wilfred Jackson
Hamilton Luske
Clyde Geronimi

From back of container

Running Time:
76 Minutes / Color
Presented in Digitally
Mastered Hi-Fi Stereo
Closed-Captioned for the hearing
impaired by Captions, Inc., Los Angeles.

WALT DISNEY HOME VIDEO
Licensed for private home exhibition only. All other rights reserved. Distributed by
Buena Vista Home Video, Burbank, California 91521. Made and printed in U.S.A.,
except cassettes distributed in Canada, duplicated in Canada. (410-1)
© MCMXLIX The Walt Disney Company.

Example 17

```
Cinderella [videorecording] / Walt Disney Pictures ; directors,
    Wilfred Jackson, Hamilton Luske, Clyde Geronimi. -- [Burbank,
    Calif.] : Walt Disney Home Video ; [distributed by Buena Vista
    Home Video], [198-]
        1 videocassette (76 min.) : sd., col. ; 1/2 in. -- (Walt
    Disney classics)

        "The original animated classic"--Container.
        Closed-captioned for the hearing impaired.
        Title on cassette: Walt Disney's Cinderella. Title on con-
    tainer: Walt Disney's classic Cinderella.
        Based on the story by Charles Perrault.
        Originally produced as motion picture in 1949.
        "Presented in digitally mastered hi-fi stereo"--Container.
        VHS.
        Rated G.
        Summary: Burdened with endless chores, Cinderella holds fast
    to dreams of some day escaping her drudgery. She goes to the ball
    with the help of her Fairy Godmother, marries the Prince, and
    lives happily ever after.
        Preceded by preview for Oliver and company.

        1. Fairy tales.  2. Children's films.  3. Animated films.  4.
    Feature films.  I. Jackson, Wilfred.  II. Luske, Hamilton.  III.
    Geronimi, Clyde.  IV. Perrault, Charles, 1628-1703. Cendrillon.
    V. Walt Disney Pictures.  VI. Walt Disney Home Video.  VII. Buena
    Vista Home Video.  VIII. Title: Walt Disney's Cinderella.  XI.
    Title: Walt Disney's classic Cinderella.  X. Series.

PN1995.9.F3
791.43637
```

Several forms of the title appear on this item.
Rule numbers for notes: 7.7B1, 7.7B2, 7.7B4, 7.7B7, 7.7B7, 7.7B10a, 7.7B10f, 7.7B14, 7.7B17, 7.7B18.

Example 17

```
Type: g     Bib lvl: m Source: d    Lang: eng
Type mat: v Enc lvl: I Govt pub:    Ctry: cau
Int lvl: g  Mod rec:   Tech: a      Leng: 076
Accomp:     MEBE: 0    Dat tp: p    Dates: 1980,1949
Desc: a
  1   010
  2   040      XXX ‡c XXX
  3   007      v ‡b f ‡d c ‡e b ‡f a ‡g h ‡h o ‡i s
  4   090      PN1995.9.F3
  5   092      791.43637 ‡2 20
  6   049      XXXX
  7   245 00 Cinderella ‡h videorecording / ‡c Walt Disney Pictures ;
directors, Wilfred Jackson, Hamilton Luske, Clyde Geronimi.
  8   260      [Burbank, Calif.] : ‡b Walt Disney Home Video ; [distrib-
uted by Buena Vista Home Video], ‡c [198-]
  9   300      1 videocassette (76 min.) : ‡b sd., col. ; ‡c 1/2 in.
 10   440  0 Walt Disney classics
 11   500      "The original animated classic"--Container.
 12   500      Closed-captioned for the hearing impaired.
 13   500      Title on cassette: Walt Disney's Cinderella. Title on con-
tainer: Walt Disney's classic Cinderella.
 14   500      Originally produced as motion picture in 1949.
 15   500      "Presented in digitally mastered hi-fi stereo"--Container.
 16   538      VHS.
 17   500      Rated G.
 18   520      Burdened with endless chores, Cinderella holds fast to
dreams of some day escaping her drudgery. She goes to the ball with the
help of her Fairy Godmother, marries the Prince, and lives happily ever
after.
 19   500      Preceded by preview for Oliver and company.
 20   650  0 Fairy tales.
 21   650  0 Children's films.
 22   650  0 Animated films.
 23   650  0 Feature films.
 24   700 11 Jackson, Wilfred.
 25   700 11 Luske, Hamilton.
 26   700 11 Geronimi, Clyde.
 27   700 11 Perrault, Charles, ‡d 1628-1703. ‡t Cendrillon.
 28   710 21 Walt Disney Pictures.
 29   710 21 Walt Disney Home Video.
 30   710 21 Buena Vista Home Video.
 31   740 01 Walt Disney's Cinderella.
 32   740 01 Walt Disney's classic Cinderella.
```

80

Example 18

Title screens

Walt Disney
Home Video
Walt Disney
Cartoon Classics
Here's Goofy!

From back of container

VOLUME 3

Here's Goofy!

Walt Disney Cartoon Classics.
A wondrous collection of cartoon masterpieces from the great Disney legacy.
Each volume in this fabulous new series is filled with the kind of joy and laughter
that have made these cartoons timeless. Yours to enjoy now ... and forever.

Goofy's wacky escapades are a treasure chest of non-stop fun!
Enjoy zillions of laughs in these three goofy gems:
▲
For Whom The Bulls Toll (1953): While visiting Mexico, El Goofy is swept
into the bullring by an adoring mob where he comes face-to-face
with his less-than-adoring opponent!
▲
Lion Down (1950): Goofy needs a second tree to support his penthouse hammock.
Problem: The fir tree he picks is home to a full-grown mountain lion!
▲
A Knight For A Day (1945): When Squire Goofy, a budding knight in armor, wants to
become *Sir* Goofy, our favorite jester turns into a jouster with questionable results!

Example 18

```
Here's Goofy! [videorecording]. -- [Burbank, Calif.] : Walt Disney
   Home Video, [1987]
      1 videocassette (22 min.) : sd., col. ; 1/2 in. -- (Walt Disney
   cartoon classics ; v. 3)

      Three animated cartoons featuring Goofy.
      Originally produced as motion pictures.
      VHS.
      Contents: For whom the bulls toil (1953) -- Lion down (1950) --
   A knight for a day (1945).

      1. Animated films.  2. Children's films.  3. Goofy (Fictitious
   character)  I. Walt Disney Home Video.  II. For whom the bulls
   toil (Motion picture).  1987.  III. Lion down (Motion picture).
   1987.  IV. Knight for a day (Motion picture).  1987.  V. Series.
```

```
PN1995.9.A53
791.533
```

This collection of three Disney cartoons has a collective title. Each cartoon was produced in a different year; I chose to add the year to each in the contents note.

The series title is given on the title frames, so is not bracketed.

The analytical added entries for the three titles listed in the contents note include the uniform title, the general material designation, and the date.

The only access we can provide for Goofy is as a subject heading (see p. 30).

Rule numbers for notes: 7.7B1, 7.7B7, 7.7B10f, 7.7B18.

```
Type: g       Bib lvl: m Source: d    Lang: eng
Type mat: v Enc lvl: I Govt pub:      Ctry: cau
Int lvl: g  Mod rec:   Tech: a        Leng: 022
Accomp:       MEBE: 0    Dat tp: s    Dates: 1987,
Desc: a
 1    010
 2    040      XXX ‡c XXX
 3    007      v ‡b f ‡d c ‡e b ‡f a ‡g h ‡h o ‡i m
 4    090      PN1995.9.A53
 5    092      791.533 ‡2 20
 6    049      XXXX
 7    245 00   Here's Goofy! ‡h videorecording
 8    260      [Burbank, Calif.] : ‡b Walt Disney Home Video, ‡c [1987]
 9    300      1 videocassette (22 min.) : ‡b sd., col. ; ‡c 1/2 in.
10    440  0   Walt Disney cartoon classics ; ‡v v. 3
11    500      Three animated cartoons featuring Goofy.
12    500      Originally produced as motion pictures.
13    538      VHS.
14    505 0    For whom the bulls toil (1953) -- Lion down (1950) -- A
knight for a day (1945).
15    650  0   Animated films.
16    650  0   Children's films.
17    650  0   Goofy (Fictitious character)
18    710 21   Walt Disney Home Video.
19    730 01   For whom the bulls toil (Motion picture). ‡f 1987.
20    730 01   Lion down (Motion picture). ‡f 1987.
21    730 01   Knight for a day (Motion picture). ‡f 1987.
```

Example 19

Title screens

Family Home Entertainment

———————

Rankin/Bass Present
Burl Ives
Tells the story of
Rudolph the
Red-Nosed Reindeer
Written by
Romeo Muller
Adapted from a story by
Robert May
and the song by
Johnny Marks
Music and Lyrics by
Johnny Marks
Co-producer
Jules Bass
Director
Larry Roemer
Produced by
Arthur Rankin, Jr.

From front of container

Christmas Classics
S · E · R · I · E · S

f.h.e.
Family Home Entertainment

SUITABLE FOR
ALL AGES

Told and Sung by BURL IVES

Example 19

```
Rudolph the red-nosed reindeer [videorecording] / Rankin/Bass ;
    produced by Arthur Rankin, Jr., co-producer, Jules Bass ; direc-
    tor, Larry Roemer ; written by Romeo Muller. -- [Van Nuys, Calif.]
    : Family Home Entertainment, [1989]
        1 videocassette (53 min.) : sd., col. ; 1/2 in. -- ([Christmas
    classics series])

        Told and sung by Burl Ives. Musical director, Maury Laws.
        "Adapted from a story by Robert May and the song by Johnny
    Marks ; music and lyrics by Johnny Marks."
        Originally produced for television in 1964.
        VHS.
        "Suitable for all ages"--Container.
        Summary: Shunned by the other reindeer because of his red nose,
    Rudolph becomes a hero when he guides Santa's sleigh through a
    blinding blizzard, and Christmas morning is saved for boys and
    girls all over the world.

        1. Christmas films.  2. Children's films.  3. Animated films.
    I. Rankin, Arthur.  II. Bass, Jules.  III. Roemer, Larry.  IV.
    Muller, Romeo.  V. Ives, Burl, 1909-  VI.  Laws, Maury.  VII.
    Marks, Johnny.  VIII. May, Robert Lewis, 1905-  Rudolph the red-
    nosed reindeer.  IX. Rankin/Bass Productions.  X. Family Home
    Entertainment.  XI. Series.

PN1995.9.C5
791.433
```

Rule numbers for notes: 7.7B6, 7.7B7, 7.7B7, 7.7B10f, 7.7B14, 7.7B17.
Date used is from the package:
   Package and Design © 1989 International Video Entertainment, Inc.
   The date is bracketed in area 4 because we assume from this information the item is published/distributed in 1989.
   The series is also bracketed because it is on the container rather than the title and credits frames.

Example 19

```
Type: g       Bib lvl: m  Source: d   Lang: eng
Type mat: v   Enc lvl: I   Govt pub:   Ctry: cau
Int lvl: g    Mod rec:     Tech: c     Leng: 053
Accomp:       MEBE: 0      Dat tp: s   Dates: 1989,
Desc: a
  1   010
  2   040       XXX   ‡c XXX
  3   007       v ‡b f ‡d c ‡e b ‡f a ‡g h ‡h o ‡i m
  4   090       PN1995.9.C5
  5   092       791.433 ‡2 20
  6   049       XXXX
  7   245 00  Rudolph the red-nosed reindeer ‡h videorecording / ‡c
Rankin/Bass ; produced by Arthur Rankin, Jr., co-producer, Jules Bass ;
director, Larry Roemer ; written by Romeo Muller.
  8   260       [Van Nuys, Calif.] : ‡b Family Home Entertainment, ‡c
[1989]
  9   300       1 videocassette (53 min.) : ‡b sd., col. ; ‡c 1/2 in.
 10   440  0  [Christmas classics series]
 11   500       Told and sung by Burl Ives. Musical director, Maury Laws.
 12   500       "Adapted from a story by Robert May and the song by Johnny
Marks. Music and lyrics by Johnny Marks."
 13   500       Originally produced for television in 1964.
 14   538       VHS.
 15   500       "Suitable for all ages"--Container.
 16   520       Shunned by the other reindeer because of his red nose,
Rudolph becomes a hero when he guides Santa's sleigh through a blinding
blizzard, and Christmas morning is saved for boys and girls all over the
world.
 17   650  0  Christmas films.
 18   650  0  Children's films.
 19   650  0  Animated films.
 20   700 11  Rankin, Arthur.
 21   700 11  Bass, Jules.
 22   700 11  Roemer, Larry.
 23   700 11  Muller, Romeo.
 24   700 11  Ives, Burl, ‡d 1909-
 25   700 11  Laws, Maury.
 26   700 11  Marks, Johnny.
 27   700 11  May, Robert Lewis, ‡d 1905- $t Rudolph the red-nosed rein-
deer.
 28   710 21  Rankin/Bass Productions.
 29   710 21  Family Home Entertainment.
```

Example 20

Title screens

ABC Video Enterprises
Rankin/Bass present
The Hobbit
c1977
Based on the original version
of The Hobbit by
JRR Tolkien
Starring in alphabetical order
Orson Bean

...

with the talents of
Paul Frees and
Jack De Leon

...

The Greatest Adventure
Ballad of the Hobbit
Sung by Glenn Yarborough
Music Composed, Arranged & Conducted
by Maury Laws
Lyrics Written & Adapted by
Jules Bass
Production Designed by
Arthur Rankin, Jr.
Adapted for the screen by
Romeo Muller

From back of container

J.R.R. TOLKIEN'S
THE
HOBBIT

1 hour 16 minutes

The copyright proprietor has licensed the
Picture contained in the videocassette for
private home use only, and prohibits any
other use, copying, reproduction, or
performance in public in whole or in part.

Example 20

```
The Hobbit [videorecording] / Rankin/Bass ; production designed by
   Arthur Rankin, Jr. ; adapted for the screen by Romeo Muller. --
   [United States] : ABC Video Enterprises ; [duplicated and distrib-
   uted by Sony Corporation of America, 198-]
       1 videocassette (76 min.) : sd., col. ; 1/2 in.

       Voices: Orson Bean, Richard Boone, Hans Conried, John Huston,
   Otto Preminger, Cyril Ritchard, Theodore ; singer, Glenn
   Yarborough.
       Credits: Music, Maury Laws ; lyrics, Jules Bass ; animation
   coordinator, Toru Hara ; animation supervisor, Tsuguyuki Kubo.
       Originally produced as motion picture for television in 1977.
   VHS.
       Summary: An animated adaptation of the book by J.R.R. Tolkien.
   Concerns the adventures of Bilbo Baggins (the Hobbit) and 13
   dwarfs as they attempt to recapture their treasure from Smaug, the
   terrible dragon.

       1. Children's films.  2. Animated films.  3. Fantastic films.
   I. Rankin, Arthur.  II. Muller, Romeo.  III. Yarborough, Glenn.
   IV. Laws, Maury.  V. Bass, Jules.  VI. Tolkien, J. R. R. (John
   Ronald Reuel), 1892-1973.  Hobbit.  VII. Rankin/Bass Productions.
   VIII. ABC Video Enterprises.

PN1995.9.F36 (fantastic films)
PR6039.O32H (Tolkien's number)
791.43615
```

Rule numbers for notes: 7.7B6a, 7.7B6b, 7.7B7, 7.7B10f, 7.7B17.

Example 20

```
Type: g      Bib lvl: m Source: d   Lang: eng
Type mat: v  Enc lvl: I Govt pub:   Ctry: en
Int lvl: g   Mod rec:   Tech: a     Leng: 076
Accomp:      MEBE: 0    Dat tp: s   Dates: 1980,
Desc: a
```

```
 1   010
 2   040      XXX ‡c XXX
 3   007      v ‡b f ‡d c ‡e b ‡f a ‡g h ‡h o ‡i m
 4   090      PN1994.9.F36 ‡a PR6039.O32H
 5   092      791.43615 ‡2 20
 6   049      XXXX
 7   245 04   The Hobbit ‡h videorecording / ‡c Rankin/Bass ; production
designed by Arthur Rankin, Jr. ; adapted for the screen by Romeo Muller.
 8   260      [United States] : ‡b ABC Video Enterprises ; ‡b [duplicated
and distributed by Sony Corporation of America, ‡c 198-]
 9   300      1 videocassette (76 min.) : ‡b sd., col. ; ‡c 1/2 in.
10   500      Voices: Orson Bean, Richard Boone, Hans Conried, John
Huston, Otto Preminger, Cyril Ritchard, Theodore ; singer, Glenn
Yarborough.
11   508      Music, Maury Laws ; lyrics, Jules Bass ; animation coordi-
nator, Toru Hara ; animation supervisor, Tsuguyuki Kubo.
12   500      Originally produced as motion picture for television in
1977.
13   538      VHS.
14   520      An animated adaptation of the book by J.R.R. Tolkien. Con-
cerns the adventures of Bilbo Baggins (the Hobbit) and 13 dwarfs as they
attempt to recapture their treasure from Smaug, the terrible dragon.
15   650  0   Children's films.
16   650  0   Animated films.
17   650  0   Fantastic films.
18   700 11   Rankin, Arthur.
19   700 11   Muller, Romeo.
20   700 11   Yarborough, Glenn.
21   700 11   Laws, Maury.
22   700 11   Bass, Jules.
23   700 11   Tolkien, J. R. R. ‡q (John Ronald Reuel), ‡d 1892-1973. ‡t
Hobbit.
24   710 21   Rankin/Bass Productions.
25   710 21   ABC Video Enterprises.
```

Example 21

Title screens

Paramount Home Video
— — — — — —

Star Trek

Created by Gene Roddenberry
Starring **William Shatner**
Also starring **Leonard Nimoy** *as Mr. Spock*
and
DeForest Kelley *as Dr. McCoy*
The Trouble with Tribbles
written by David Gerrold
Produced by
Gene L. Coon
Directed by
Joseph Pevney

Side of container

Example 21

```
The Trouble with Tribbles [videorecording] / produced by Gene L. Coon
   ; directed by Joseph Pevney ; written by David Gerrold. -- [Los
   Angeles, Calif.] : Paramount Home Video, [1980]
      1 videocassette (50 min.) : sd., col. ; 1/2 in. -- ([Star trek
   ; episode 42])

      Cast: William Shatner, Leonard Nimoy, DeForest Kelley, William
   Schallert, William Koloth.
      Created by Gene Roddenberry.
      Originally produced for television in 1967; air date, Dec. 29,
   1967.
      VHS hi-fi.
      Summary: "The Enterprise receives a top priority order to
   protect Space Station K-7 ... Involved in a running quarrel with
   both the Federation Undersecretary for Agriculture and the Klingon
   Commander, Captain Kirk fails to notice the sudden popularity of a
   new fad--Tribbles"--Container.

      1. Science fiction films.  I. Coon, Gene L.  II. Pevney, Jo-
   seph.  III. Gerrold, David, 1944-  IV. Shatner, William.  V.
   Nimoy, Leonard, 1936-  VI. Kelley, DeForest, 1920-  VII.
   Schallert, William, 1925-  VIII. Koloth, William.  IX.
   Roddenberry, Gene.  X. Paramount Home Video.  XI. Series: Star
   trek (Television program) ; episode 42.


PN1995.9.S694
791.456356
```

This is one episode of a television series. The summary is quoted from the container.
The series is bracketed because that information comes from the container.
Rule numbers for notes: 7.7B6a, 7.7B6b, 7.7B7, 7.7B10f, 7.7B17.

Example 21

```
Type: g       Bib lvl: m Source: d   Lang: eng
Type mat: v Enc lvl: I Govt pub:   Ctry: cau
Int lvl: g  Mod rec:   Tech: l     Leng: 050
Accomp:     MEBE: 0    Dat tp: s   Dates: 1980,
Desc: a
  1   010
  2   040      XXX ‡c XXX
  3   007      v ‡b f ‡d c ‡e b ‡f a ‡g h ‡h o ‡i m
  4   090      PN1995.9.S694
  5   092      791.456356 ‡2 20
  6   049      XXXX
  7   245 04   The Trouble with Tribbles ‡h videorecording / ‡c produced by
Gene L. Coon ; directed by Joseph Pevney ; written by David Gerrold.
  8   260      [Los Angeles, Calif.] : ‡b Paramount Home Video, ‡c [1980]
  9   300      1 videocassette (50 min.) : ‡b sd., col. ; ‡c 1/2 in.
 10   490 1    [Star trek ; ‡v episode 42]
 11   511 1    William Shatner, Leonard Nimoy, DeForest Kelley, William
Schallert, William Koloth.
 12   500      Created by Gene Roddenberry.
 13   500      Originally produced for television in 1967; air date, Dec. 29,
1967.
 14   538      VHS hi-fi.
 15   520      "The Enterprise receives a top priority order to protect Space
Station K-7 ... Involved in a running quarrel with both the Federation
Undersecretary for Agriculture and the Klingon Commander, Captain Kirk fails
to notice the sudden popularity of a new fad--Tribbles"--Container.
 16   650  0   Science fiction films.
 17   700 11   Coon, Gene L.
 18   700 11   Pevney, Joseph.
 19   700 11   Gerrold, David, ‡d 1944-
 20   700 11   Shatner, William.
 21   700 11   Nimoy, Leonard, ‡d 1936-
 22   700 11   Kelley, DeForest, ‡d 1920-
 23   700 11   Schallert, William, ‡d 1925-
 24   700 11   Koloth, William.
 25   700 11   Roddenberry, Gene.
 26   710 21   Paramount Home Video.
 27   830  0   Star Trek (Television program) ; ‡v episode 42.
```

Example 22

Title screens

Paramount Home Video
———————

Paramount Pictures Presents
A Gene Roddenberry Production
A Robert Wise Film

Star Trek ™

The Motion Picture
Starring
William Shatner
Leonard Nimoy
DeForest Kelley
Co-Starring
James Doohan
George Takei
Walter Koenig
Nichelle Nichols
Majel Barrett
Presenting
Persis Khambatta
and starring
Stephen Collins
as Decker
Music by
Jerry Goldsmith
Edited by
Todd Ramsay
Based on Star Trek created by
Gene Roddenberry
Screenplay by
Harold Livingston
Story by
Alan Dean Foster
Produced by
Gene Roddenberry
Directed by
Robert Wise

92

Example 22

Front of container

Example 22

```
Star trek (Motion picture : Special longer version)
    Star trek [videorecording] : the motion picture / Paramount Pic-
tures ; produced by Gene Roddenberry ; directed by Robert Wise ;
screenplay by Harold Livingston. -- [Special longer version]. --
[Hollywood, CA] : Paramount Home Video, [1983]
    1 videocassette (143 min.) : sd., col. ; 1/2 in.

    Cast: William Shatner, Leonard Nimoy, DeForest Kelley, James
Doohan, George Takei, Walter Koenig, Nichelle Nichols, Majel Barrett,
Persis Khambatta, Stephen Collins.
    Music by Jerry Goldsmith.
    Story by Alan Dean Foster, based on the television program Star
trek, created by Gene Roddenberry.
    Originally produced as motion picture in 1980.
    "Stereo, Dolby system"--Container.
    VHS.
    Rated G.
    Summary: When an unidentified alien destroys three powerful
Klingon cruisers, Capt. James T. Kirk and the cast from the Star trek
television series return to the newly transformed U.S.S. Enterprise
to stop the alien intruder from its relentless flight toward Earth.

    1. Science fiction films.  2. Feature films.  I. Roddenberry,
Gene.  II. Wise, Robert.  III. Livingston, Harold.  IV. Shatner,
William.  V. Nimoy, Leonard, 1936-  VI. Kelley, DeForest, 1920-  VII.
Doohan, James.  VIII. Takei, George, 1940-  IX. Koenig, Walter.  X.
Nichols, Nichelle.  XI. Barrett, Majel.  XII. Khambatta, Persis.
XIII. Collins, Stephen.  XIV. Goldsmith, Jerry.  XV. Foster, Alan
Dean, 1946-  XVI. Paramount Pictures Corporation.  XVII. Paramount
Home Video.  XVIII. Star trek (Television program)  XIX. Title: Star
trek, the motion picture.

PN1995.9.S694
791.436356
```

This film is based on the earlier television series. A uniform title main entry is used, assuming conflict in my catalog. A uniform title added entry is used for the television program on which this is based.

The edition statement is bracketed because it comes from the container.

Rule numbers for notes: 7.7B6a, 7.7B6b, 7.7B6b combined with 7.7B7, 7.7B7, 7.7B10a, 7.7B10f, 7.7B14, 7.7B17.

Example 22

```
Type: g      Bib lvl: m Source: d   Lang: eng
Type mat: v Enc lvl: I Govt pub:    Ctry: cau
Int lvl: g  Mod rec:   Tech: l      Leng: 143
Accomp:     MEBE: 0    Dat tp: s    Dates: 1983,
Desc: a
  1   010
  2   040
  3   007     v ‡b f ‡d c ‡e b ‡f a ‡g h ‡h o ‡i s
  4   090     PN1995.9.S694
  5   092     791.436356 ‡2 20
  6   049     XXXX
  7   130 0   Star trek (Motion picture : Special longer version)
  8   245 00  Star trek ‡h videorecording : ‡b the motion picture / ‡c
Paramount Pictures ; produced by Gene Roddenberry ; directed by Robert
Wise ; screenplay by Harold Livingston.
  9   250     [Special longer version].
 10   260     Hollywood, CA : ‡b Paramount Home Video, ‡c 1983.
 11   300     1 videocassette (143 min.) : ‡b sd., col. ; ‡c 1/2 in.
 12   511 1   William Shatner, Leonard Nimoy, DeForest Kelley, James
Doohan, George Takei, Walter Koenig, Nichelle Nichols, Majel Barrett,
Persis Khambatta, Stephen Collins.
 13   500     Music by Jerry Goldsmith.
 14   500     Story by Alan Dean Foster, based on the television program
Star trek, created by Gene Roddenberry.
 15   500     Originally produced as motion picture in 1980.
 16   500     "Stereo, Dolby system"--Container.
 17   538     VHS.
 18   500     Rated G.
 19   520     When an unidentified alien destroys three powerful Klingon
cruisers, Capt. James T. Kirk and the cast from the Star trek television
series return to the newly transformed U.S.S. Enterprise to stop the
alien intruder from its relentless flight toward Earth.
 20   650 0   Science fiction films.
 21   650 0   Feature films.
 22   700 11  Roddenberry, Gene.
 23   700 11  Wise, Robert.
 24   700 11  Livingston, Harold.
 25   700 11  Shatner, William.
 26   700 11  Nimoy, Leonard, ‡d 1936-
 27   700 11  Kelley, DeForest, ‡d 1920-
 28   700 11  Doohan, James.
 29   700 11  Takei, George, ‡d 1940-
 30   700 11  Koenig, Walter.
 31   700 11  Nichols, Nichelle.
 32   700 11  Barrett, Majel.
 33   700 11  Khambatta, Persis.
 34   700 11  Collins, Stephen.
 35   700 11  Goldsmith, Jerry.
 36   700 11  Foster, Alan Dean, ‡d 1946-
 37   710 21  Paramount Pictures Corporation.
 38   710 21  Paramount Home Video.
 39   730 01  Star trek (Television program)
 40   740 01  Star trek, the motion picture.
```

Example 23

Title screens

CBS/Fox Video
— — — — —
Twentieth Century-Fox
Presents
A
Lucasfilm Limited
Production
A long time ago in a galaxy
far far away ...

STAR

WARS

Episode IV
A New Hope

[at beginning of film]
————————
[at end of film]

Written and Directed by
George Lucas
Produced by
Gary Kurtz
Starring
Mark Hamill
Carrie Fisher
Harrison Ford
and
Alec Guinness
with
...
Music by
John Williams
Performed by the London Symphony Orchestra

Example 23

From back of container

PG PARENTAL GUIDANCE SUGGESTED
SOME MATERIAL MAY NOT BE SUITABLE FOR CHILDREN

Motion Picture Copyright © 1977 Twentieth
Century-Fox Film Corporation.
ALL RIGHTS RESERVED.
* TM: Trademark owned by Lucasfilm Ltd.

⊏ CLOSED CAPTIONED by National Captioning
Institute. Used with Permission.

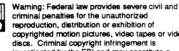 Only factory sealed pakages
contain this mark on wrapper.

Mono Compatible.

Except in Canada CBS™ is a trademark of CBS Inc. used under license.
In Canada CBS™ is a trademark of CBS Records Canada Ltd. used under license.
FOX™ is a trademark of Twentieth Century-Fox Film Corporation used under license.
Packaging Copyright © 1984 CBS/FOX
Company and Lucasfilm Ltd. (LFL) All Rights Reserved.
CBS/FOX VIDEO
Industrial Park Drive
Farmington Hills, Michigan 48024

Warning: Federal law provides severe civil and criminal penalties for the unauthorized reproduction, distribution or exhibition of copyrighted motion pictures, video tapes or video discs. Criminal copyright infringement is investigated by the FBI and may constitute a felony with a maximum penalty of up to five years in prison and/or a $250,000 fine.

```
Star wars.  Episode IV,  A new hope [videorecording] / Twentieth
   Century-Fox ; written and directed by George Lucas ; produced by
   Gary Kurtz. -- [Farmington Hills, Mich.] : CBS/Fox Video, [1984]
      1 videocassette (121 min.) : sd., col. ; 1/2 in.

      Closed-captioned for the hearing impaired.
      Cast: Mark Hamill, Harrison Ford, Carrie Fisher, Peter Cushing,
   Alec Guinness, David Prowse.
      "Music by John Williams, performed by the London Symphony
   Orchestra."
      Originally produced as motion picture in 1977.
      "Hi-fi stereo, digitally mastered"--Container.
      VHS.
      Rated PG.
      Summary: Princess Leia is captured and held hostage by the evil
   Imperial forces in their effort to take over the galactic Empire.
   Luke Skywalker, Han Solo, and two robots (R2-D2 and C-3PO) work
   together to rescue the princess and restore justice in the Empire.

      1. Science fiction films.  2. Feature films.  3. Films for the
   hearing impaired.  I. Lucas, George.  II. Kurtz, Gary.  III.
   Hamill, Mark.  IV. Ford, Harrison, 1942-  V. Fisher, Carrie.  VI.
   Cushing, Peter, 1913-  VII. Guinness, Alec, 1914-  VIII. Prowse,
   David.  IX. Williams, John, 1932-  X. Twentieth Century-Fox Film
   Corporation.  XI. CBS/Fox Video.  XII. London Symphony Orchestra.
   XIII. Title: New hope.

PN1995.9.S26
791.436356
```

Example 23

Notice the wording on the title screens indicating this is one episode in a longer work.
Rule numbers for notes: 7.7B2, 7.7B6a, 7.7B6b, 7.7B7, 7.7B10a, 7.7B10f, 7.7B14, 7.7B17.
The date comes from the package copyright date. This is assumed to be the date of distribution.

```
Type: g      Bib lvl: m Source: d   Lang: eng
Type mat: v Enc lvl: I Govt pub:    Ctry: enk
Int lvl: g  Mod rec:   Tech: l      Leng: 121
Accomp:     MEBE: 0    Dat tp: p    Dates: 1984,1977
Desc: a
  1   010
  2   040     XXX ‡c XXX
  3   007     v ‡b f ‡d c ‡e b ‡f a ‡g h ‡h o ‡i s
  4   090     PN1995.9.S26
  5   092     791.436356 ‡2 20
  6   049     XXXX
  7   245 00  Star wars. ‡n Episode IV, ‡p A new hope ‡h videorecording /
‡c Twentieth Century-Fox ; written and directed by George Lucas ; pro-
duced by Gary Kurtz.
  8   260     [Farmington Hills, Mich.] : ‡b CBS/Fox Video, ‡c [1984]
  9   300     1 videocassette (121 min.) : ‡b sd., col. ; ‡c 1/2 in.
 10   500     Closed-captioned for the hearing impaired.
 11   511 1   Mark Hamill, Harrison Ford, Carrie Fisher, Peter Cushing,
Alec Guinness, David Prowse.
 12   500     "Music by John Williams, performed by the London Symphony
Orchestra."
 13   500     Originally produced as motion picture in 1977.
 14   500     "Hi-fi stereo, digitally mastered"--Container.
 15   538     VHS.
 16   500     Rated PG.
 17   520     Princess Leia is captured and held hostage by the evil
Imperial forces in their effort to take over the galactic Empire. Luke
Skywalker, Han Solo, and two robots (R2-D2 and C-3PO) work together to
rescue the princess and restore justice in the Empire.
 18   650 0   Science fiction films.
 19   650 0   Feature films.
 20   650 0   Films for the hearing impaired.
 21   700 11  Lucas, George.
 22   700 11  Kurtz, Gary.
 23   700 11  Hamill, Mark.
 24   700 11  Ford, Harrison, ‡d 1942-
 25   700 11  Fisher, Carrie.
 26   700 11  Cushing, Peter, ‡d 1913-
 27   700 11  Guinness, Alec, ‡d 1914-
 28   700 11  Prowse, David.
 29   700 11  Williams, John, ‡d 1932-
 30   710 21  Twentieth Century-Fox Film Corporation.
 31   710 21  CBS/Fox Video.
 32   710 21  London Symphony Orchestra.
 33   740 01  New hope.
```

98

Example 24

Title screens

from
WTVS Detroit
[funding sources]
The National
Endowment for the Humanities
The
Arthur Vining Davis
Foundation
The Jack
and Charlotte
Lehrman Foundation
—
Unicorn Projects
A Unicorn Project
Based on the book by
David Macauley
with David Macaulay
and Sarah Bullen

Castle

A
Unicorn
Project
Executive Producer
Ray Hubbard
Producers
Larry Klein
Mark Olshaker
Written by
Mark Olshaker
Animation by
The Animation
Partnership
In Association With
TV Cartoons, Ltd.
Director
Jack Stokes
Producer
John Coates
Live Action Sequences
by
Carl Gover
Associates
Producers
Colin Leighton
Director
Peter Newington
c1983

Example 24

```
Castle [videorecording] / Unicorn Projects ; producers, Larry Klein,
   Mark Olshaker ; written by Mark Olshaker. -- [England? : Dorset
   Video], c1983.
      1 videocassette (58 min.) : sd., col. ; 1/2 in.

      Animation by the Animation Partnership in association with TV
   Cartoons, Ltd. ; director, Jack Stokes ; producer, John Coates.
   Live action sequences by Carl Gover Associates ; producer, Colin
   Leighton ; director, Peter Newington.
      Based on the book by David Macaulay.
      Originally produced for public television.
      VHS.
      Summary: An animated tale about a fictional thirteenth-century
   fortress and town built by King Edward I to subdue the Welsh.
   Includes live-action sequences in which David Macaulay and Sarah
   Bullen explain the history and architecture that inspired the
   fictional castle.

      1. Castles.  2. Fortification.  3. Middle Ages.  I. Klein,
   Larry.  II. Olshaker, Mark, 1951-  III. Macaulay, David.  Castle.
   IV. Unicorn Projects.  V. Dorset Video.

   UG405
   623
```

This production has credits for the animated portions, credits for the live portions, and credits for the total production. I hope I have them straightened out correctly. I did not make added entries for any other than those having responsibility for the total production.

Rule numbers for notes: 7.7B6b, 7.7B7, 7.7B7, 7.7B10f, 7.7B17.

Example 24

```
Type: g      Bib lvl: m Source: d    Lang: eng
Type mat: v  Enc lvl: I Govt pub:    Ctry: enk
Int lvl: e   Mod rec:   Tech: c      Leng: 058
Accomp:      MEBE: 0    Dat tp: s    Dates: 1983
Desc: a
 1   010
 2   040      XXX ‡c XXX
 3   007      v ‡b f ‡d c ‡e b ‡f a ‡g h ‡h o ‡i m
 4   043      e-uk-wl
 5   090      UG405
 6   092      623 ‡2 20
 7   049      XXXX
 8   245 00   Castle ‡h videorecording / ‡c Unicorn Projects ; producers,
Larry Klein, Mark Olshaker ; written by Mark Olshaker.
 9   260      [England? : ‡b Dorset Video], ‡c c1983.
10   300      1 videocassette (58 min.) : ‡b sd., col. ; ‡c 1/2 in.
11   500      Animation by the Animation Partnership in association with
TV Cartoons, Ltd. ; director, Jack Stokes ; producer, John Coates. Live
action sequences by Carl Gover Associates ; producer, Colin Leighton ;
director, Peter Newington.
12   500      Originally produced for public television.
13   500      Based on the book by David Macaulay.
14   538      VHS.
15   520      An animated tale about a fictional thirteenth-century for-
tress and town built by King Edward I to subdue the Welsh. Includes
live-action sequences in which David Macaulay and Sarah Bullen explain
the history and architecture that inspired the fictional castle.
16   650  0   Castles.
17   650  0   Fortification.
18   650  0   Middle Ages.
19   700 11   Klein, Larry.
20   700 11   Olshaker, Mark, ‡d 1951-
21   700 11   Macaulay, David. ‡t Castle.
22   710 21   Unicorn Projects.
23   710 21   Dorset Video.
```

Example 25

Front of container

Example 25

Title screens

Produced-Written-Directed
by
Michael R. Barnard
Music Composed & Performed
by
The Castle Family
A Production of
Kjell Bergh
for
Matt Blair's Celebrity Promotions
c1987.

```
The Berenguer boogie [videorecording] / a production of Kjell Bergh
    for Matt Blair's Celebrity Promotions ; produced, written, di-
    rected by Michael R. Barnard. -- [Plymouth, Minn. : Simitar Enter-
    tainment], c1987.
        1 videocassette (12 min.) : sd., col. ; 1/2 in. + 1 poster
    (col. ; 45 x 29 cm.)

        Title from container.
        "Starring Juan Berenguer of the Twins [with] Tony Oliva, Al
    Newman, Les Straker"--Container.
        Music composed and performed by the Castle Family.
        VHS hi-fi, stereo.
        Summary: A musical tribute to Berenguer, Minnesota Twins relief
    pitcher, after his winning performance in the 1987 American League
    championship series. Music video is followed by KSTP-TV news
    report on the making of the video.

        1. Berenguer, Juan, 1954-  2. Minnesota Twins (Baseball team)
    3.  Baseball--Minnesota.  4. Television--Production and direction.
    5. Berenguer boogie.  I. Bergh, Kjell.  II. Barnard, Michael R.
    III. Castle Family (Musical group)  IV. Matt Blair's Celebrity
    Promotions, Inc.  V. KSTP-TV (Television station : Saint Paul,
    Minn.)  VI. Simitar Entertainment.

GV865.B4
796.75722
```

Rule numbers for notes: 7.7B4, 7.7B6a, 7.7B6b, 7.7B10f and a combined, 7.7B17.
The title does not appear anywhere on the title screens.
The subject heading for "Berenguer boogie" is added because the news report about the making of it is included in the videocassette.

Example 25

```
Type: g       Bib lvl: m Source: d    Lang: eng
Type mat: v Enc lvl: I Govt pub:      Ctry: mnu
Int lvl: e  Mod rec:   Tech: l        Leng: 012
Accomp:     MEBE: 0    Dat tp: s      Dates: 1987,
Desc: a
 1   010
 2   040       XXX ‡c XXX
 3   007       v ‡b f ‡d c ‡e b ‡f a ‡g h ‡h o ‡i m
 4   043       n-us-mn
 5   090       GV865.B4
 6   092       796.35722 ‡2 20
 7   049       XXXX
 8   245 04    The Berenguer boogie ‡h videorecording / ‡c a production of
Kjell Bergh for Matt Blair's Celebrity Promotions ; produced, written,
directed by Michael R. Barnard.
 9   260       [Plymouth, Minn. : ‡b Simitar Entertainment], ‡c c1987.
10   300       1 videocassette (12 min.) : ‡b sd., col. ; ‡c 1/2 in. + ‡e
1 poster (col. ; 45 x 29 cm.)
11   500       Title from container.
12   500       "Starring Juan Berenguer of the Twins [with] Tony Oliva, Al
Newman, Les Straker"--Container.
13   500       Music composed and performed by the Castle Family.
14   538       VHS hi-fi, stereo.
15   520       A musical tribute to Berenguer, Minnesota Twins relief
pitcher, after his winning performance in the 1987 American League
championship series. Music video is followed by KSTP-TV news report on
the making of the video.
16   600 10    Berenguer, Juan, ‡d 1954-
17   610 20    Minnesota Twins (Baseball team).
18   650  0    Baseball ‡z Minnesota.
19   650  0    Television ‡x Production and direction.
20   630 00    Berenguer boogie.
21   700 11    Bergh, Kjell.
22   700 11    Barnard, Michael R.
23   710 21    Castle Family (Musical group)
24   710 21    Matt Blair's Celebrity Promotions, Inc.
25   710 21    KSTP-TV (Television station : Saint Paul, Minn.)
26   710 21    Simitar Entertainment.
```

Example 26

Title screens

CBS/Fox Video
———————

Major League Baseball
Productions
ABC Sports

<table>
<tr><td></td><td align="right">1987
World
Series</td></tr>
<tr><td>... There's no place
like home</td><td></td></tr>
</table>

Example 26

    --There's no place like home [videorecording] : 1987 world series /
       ABC Sports ; Major League Baseball Productions. -- [Livonia,
       Mich.] : CBS/Fox Video, c1987.
          1 videocassette (50 min.) : sd., col. ; 1/2 in.

       "The official World Series video"--Container.
       Narrator: Al Michaels.
       VHS.
       Summary: Highlights of the 1987 World Series games between the
    St. Louis Cardinals and the winning team, the Minnesota Twins.

       1. World series (Baseball) 2. Minnesota Twins (Baseball team)
    3. St. Louis Cardinals (Baseball team) I. Michaels, Al. II. ABC
    Sports. III. Major League Baseball Productions. IV. CBS/Fox
    Video.

    GV875.A1
    796.357646

Rule numbers for notes: 7.7B1, 7.7B6b, 7.7B10f, 7.7B17.
The "..." preceding "There's" is replaced by "--" on the basis of rule 1.1B1.

Type: g   Bib lvl: m Source: d   Lang: eng
Type mat: v Enc lvl: I Govt pub: Ctry: us
Int lvl: e Mod rec: Tech: 1   Leng: 050
Accomp: MEBE: 0   Dat tp: s   Dates: 1987
Desc: a
  1   010
  2   040   XXX ‡c XXX
  3   007   v ‡b f ‡d c ‡e b ‡f a ‡g h ‡h o ‡i s
  4   090   GV875.A1
  5   092   796.35746 ‡2 20
  6   049   XXXX
  7   245 00   --There's no place like home ‡h videorecording : ‡b 1987
world series / ‡c ABC Sports ; Major League Baseball Productions.
  8   260   [Livonia, Mich.] : ‡b CBS/Fox Video, ‡c c1987.
  9   300   1 videocassette (50 min.) : ‡b sd., col. ; ‡c 1/2 in.
 10   500   "The official World Series video"--Container.
 11   511 1   Al Michaels.
 12   538   VHS.
 13   520   Highlights of the 1987 World Series games between the St.
Louis Cardinals and the winning team, the Minnesota Twins.
 14   650 0 World series (Baseball)
 15   610 20 Minnesota Twins (Baseball team)
 16   610 20 St. Louis Cardinals (Baseball team)
 17   700 11 Michaels, Al.
 18   710 21 ABC Sports.
 19   710 21 Major League Baseball Productions.
 20   710 21 CBS/Fox Video.

Example 27

Title screens

The Durango & Silverton Narrow Gauge Railroad
Produced by Western Audio-Visual
Durango, Colorado
c1987

[Above are the total credits appearing on the film. There is little narration. Captions give name of feature with milepost number.]

Front of container

Example 27

```
The Durango & Silverton Narrow Gauge Railroad [videorecording] /
    produced by Western Audio-Visual. -- Durango, Colo. : Western
    Audio-Visual, c1987.
        1 videocassette (55 min.) : sd., col. ; 1/2 in.

        Title on container: Coal smoke & steam : Durango to Silverton
    on the narrow gauge.
        VHS.
        Summary: As viewer travels the route of the Durango & Silverton
    Narrow Gauge Railroad, captions give names of the features shown,
    while mile post markers indicate the exact location. Minimal
    narration.

        1. Durango and Silverton Narrow Gauge Railroad--History.  2.
    Railroads, Narrow-gage--Colorado--History.  I. Western Audio-
    Visual.  II. Title: Coal smoke & steam.

    TF24.C62D8
    385.52
```

This video had totally different titles on the film and on the container.
Rule numbers for notes: 7.7B4, 7.7B10f, 7.7B17.

```
Type: g       Bib lvl: m Source: d   Lang: eng
Type mat: v Enc lvl: I Govt pub:     Ctry: cou
Int lvl: f  Mod rec:    Tech: 1      Leng: 024
Accomp:     MEBE: 0     Dat tp: s    Dates: 1987,
Desc: a
 1    010
 2    040     XXX ǂc XXX
 3    007     v ǂb f ǂd c ǂe b ǂf a ǂg h ǂh o ǂi m
 4    043     n-us-co
 5    090     TF24.C62 ǂb D8
 6    092     385.52 ǂ2 20
 7    049     XXXX
 8    245 04  The Durango & Silverton Narrow Gauge Railroad ǂh
videorecording / ǂc produced by Western Audio-Visual.
 9    260     Durango, Colo. : ǂb Western Audio-Visual, ǂc c1987.
10    300     1 videocassette (55 min.) : ǂb sd., col. ; ǂc 1/2 in.
11    500     Title on container: Coal smoke & steam : Durango to
Silverton on the narrow gauge.
12    538     VHS.
13    520     As viewer travels the route of the Durango & Silverton
Narrow Gauge Railroad, captions give names of the features shown, while
mile post markers indicate the exact location. Minimal narration.
14    610 20  Durango and Silverton Narrow Gauge Railroad ǂx History.
15    650  0  Railroads, Narrow-gage ǂz Colorado ǂx History.
16    710 21  Western Audio-Visual.
17    740 01  Coal smoke & steam.
```

Example 28

Title screens

MEDIA 7
The
Minnesota State
College System
Presents …
Death and Dying
Elisabeth Kübler-Ross
M.D.
General Attitudes
Children
Producer-Moderator
Rita Shaw
Director
Denny Spence
Produced by KTCA-TV

Example 28

```
Death and dying [videorecording] / Minnesota State College System ;
   produced by KTCA-TV ; director, Denny Spence ; producer-moderator,
   Rita Shaw. -- [1974]
        1 videocassette (57 min.) : sd., col. ; 3/4 in.

        Recorded off-air May 1974 by Mankato State College, with per-
   mission of KTCA-TV.
        Summary: Psychiatrist Elisabeth Kübler-Ross discusses tech-
   niques to help one prepare for and accept death as a part of life.
        Contents: General attitudes (27 min.) -- Children (30 min.).

        1. Death.  I. Spence, Denny.  II. Shaw, Rita.  III. Kübler-
   Ross, Elisabeth.  IV. Minnesota State College System.  V. KTCA-TV
   (Television station : Saint Paul, Minn.)
```

```
BF789.D4
155.937
```

This example shows how to handle something recorded (legally) off-air.
Rule numbers for notes: 7.7B9, 7.7B17, 7.7B18.
In this format "Ctry" is coded for the country of *production* rather than *publication*. An unpublished work is coded.

```
Type: g      Bib lvl: m Source: d    Lang: eng
Type mat: v Enc lvl: I Govt pub:    Ctry: mnu
Int lvl: e  Mod rec:   Tech: l      Leng: 057
Accomp:      MEBE: 0     Dat tp: s   Dates: 1974
Desc: a
  1   010
  2   040      XXX ǂc XXX
  3   007      v ǂb f ǂd c ǂe c ǂf a ǂg h ǂh r ǂi m
  4   090      BF789.D4
  5   092      155.937 ǂ2 20
  6   049      XXXX
  7   245 00 Death and dying $h videorecording / ǂc Minnesota State
College System ; produced by KTCA-TV ; director, Denny Spence ; pro-
ducer-moderator, Rita Shaw.
  8   260      ǂc [1974]
  9   300      1 videocassette (57 min.) : ǂb sd., col. ; ǂc 3/4 in.
 10   500      Recorded off-air May 1974 by Mankato State College, with
permission of KTCA-TV.
 11   520      Psychiatrist Elisabeth Kübler-Ross discusses techniques to
help one prepare for and accept death as a part of life.
 12   505 0  General attitudes (27 min.) -- Children (30 min.).
 13   650  0  Death.
 14   700 11 Spence, Denny.
 15   700 11 Shaw, Rita.
 16   700 21 Kübler-Ross, Elisabeth.
 17   710 21 Minnesota State College System.
 18   710 21 KTCA-TV (Television station : Saint Paul, Minn.)
```

Example 29A
These examples show a set of videos cataloged as a unit, and one of the set cataloged individually.

Title screens

DISTRIBUTED BY
TIME-LIFE FILMS
————

LIFE
GOES TO THE
MOVIES
————

A PRESENTATION OF
20th CENTURY-FOX
TELEVISION
AND
TIME-LIFE TELEVISION
————

Executive Producer
JACK HALEY, JR.
————

Produced by
MEL STUART
and
RICHARD SCHICKEL
————

Directed by
MEL STUART
————

Written by
RICHARD SCHICKEL
————

Original Music Composed
and Conducted by
FRED KARLIN

Original Music Copyright © 1976 Twentieth Century Music Corporation

Example 29A

Life goes to the movies [videorecording] / a presentation of 20th
   Century-Fox Television and Time-Life Television ; executive pro-
   ducer, Jack Haley, Jr. ; produced by Mel Stuart and Richard
   Schickel ; directed by Mel Stuart ; written by Richard Schickel.
   -- [Paramus, N.J.] : Time-Life Films, 1976.
      5 videocassettes (165 min.) : sd., col. with b&w sequences ;
   3/4 in.

      Narrators: Henry Fonda, Shirley MacLaine, Liza Minnelli.
      Also issued as motion pictures.
      Summary: A compilation of feature film clips, news photographs
from Life magazine, and narrative that examines the development of
20th century American popular culture as reflected in motion
pictures and in Life magazine.
      Contents: pt. 1. The golden age of Hollywood [Title on con-
tainer: Golden years of Hollywood] (35 min.) -- pt. 2. The war
years (33 min.) -- pt. 3. The post war era [Title on container:
Post-war years] (20 min.) -- pt. 4. The fifties (28 min., 30 sec.)
-- pt. 5. The new morality [Title on container: Movies today](39
min.).

      1. Motion pictures--United States--History. I. Haley, Jack.
II. Stuart, Mel. III. Schickel, Richard. IV. Fonda, Henry, 1905-
V. MacLaine, Shirley. VI. Minnelli, Liza. VII. 20th Century-Fox
Television. VIII. Time-Life Television. IX. Time-Life Films. X.
Life (Chicago, Ill. : 1935) XI. Golden age of Hollywood. 1976.
XII. War years. 1976. XIII. Post war era. 1976. XIV. Fifties.
1976. XV. New morality. 1976. XVI. Title: Golden years of Holly-
wood. XVII. Title: Post-war years. XVIII. Title: Movies today.

PN1993.5.U6
791.43

Rule numbers for notes: 7.7B6a, 7.7B14, 7.7B17, 7.7B18.
Following the LCRI for 1.7B18 (*CSB* 49), "pt." following "Contents" is not capitalized.
   The analytical entries are traced in uniform title form. The added entries for titles traced differently are not uniform titles.

Example 29A

```
Type: g      Bib lvl: m Source: d   Lang: eng
Type mat: v Enc lvl: I Govt pub:    Ctry: xxu
Int lvl: g  Mod rec:   Tech: a      Leng: 165
Accomp:     MEBE: 0    Dat tp: s    Dates: 1976,
Desc: a
  1   010
  2   040     XXX ǂc XXX
  3   007     v ǂb f ǂd m ǂd c ǂf a ǂg h ǂh r ǂi m
  4   043     n-us—
  5   045     x2x7
  6   090     PN1993.5.U6
  7   092     791.43 ǂ2
  8   049     XXXX
  9   245 00  Life goes to the movies ǂh videorecording / ǂc a presenta-
tion of 20th Century-Fox Television and Time-Life Television ; execu-
tive producer, Jack Haley, Jr. ; produced by Mel Stuart and Richard
Schickel ; directed by Mel Stuart ; written by Richard Schickel.
 10   260     [Paramus, N.J.] : ǂb Time-Life Films, ǂc 1976.
 11   300     5 videocassettes (165 min.) : ǂb sd., col. with b&w se-
quences ; ǂc 3/4 in.
 12   511 0   Narrators: Henry Fonda, Shirley MacLaine, Liza Minnelli.
 13   500     Also issued as motion pictures.
 14   520     A compilation of feature film clips, news photographs from
Life magazine, and narrative that examines the development of 20th
century American popular culture as reflected in motion pictures and in
Life magazine.
 15   505 0   pt. 1. The golden age of Hollywood [Title on container:
Golden years of Hollywood] (35 min.) -- pt. 2. The war years (33 min.)
-- pt. 3. The post war era [Title on container: Post-war years] (20
min.) -- pt. 4. The fifties (28 min., 30 sec.) -- pt. 5. The new moral-
ity [Title on container: Movies today](39 min.).
 16   650 0   Motion pictures ǂz United States ǂx History.
 17   700 11  Haley, Jack.
 18   700 11  Stuart, Mel.
 19   700 11  Schickel, Richard.
 20   700 11  Fonda, Henry, ǂd 1905-
 21   700 11  MacLaine, Shirley.
 22   700 11  Minnelli, Liza.
 23   710 21  20th Century-Fox Television.
 24   710 21  Time-Life Television.
 25   710 21  Time-Life Films.
 26   730 01  Life (Chicago, Ill. : 1935)
 27   730 01  Golden age of Hollywood. ǂf 1976.
 28   730 01  War years. ǂf 1976.
 29   730 01  Post war era. ǂf 1976.
 30   730 01  Fifties. ǂf 1976.
 31   730 01  New morality. ǂf 1976.
 32   740 01  Golden years of Hollywood.
 33   740 01  Post-war years.
 34   740 01  Movies today.
```

In line 12, the code 511 with first indicator 3 would generate "Narrator:". We want the plural "Narrators:" so must input that word as needed. The code 511 with first indicator 0 does not generate any print constant.

Example 29 B

Title screens

THE GOLDEN AGE OF HOLLYWOOD

———

THE WAR YEARS

———

THE POST WAR ERA

———

The Fifties

———

The New Morality

———

Hosted by HENRY FONDA
SHIRLEY MacLAINE
LIZA MINELLI

Container labels

LIFE GOES TO THE MOVIES
GOLDEN YEARS OF HOLLYWOOD
35:00 minutes

LIFE GOES TO THE MOVIES
WAR YEARS
33:00 minutes

LIFE GOES TO THE MOVIES
POST-WAR YEARS
20:00 minutes

LIFE GOES TO THE MOVIES
THE FIFTIES
28:30 minutes

LIFE GOES TO THE MOVIES
MOVIES TODAY
39:00 minutes

Example 29B

> The New morality [videorecording] / a presentation of 20th Century-
> Fox Television and Time-Life Television ; executive producer, Jack
> Haley, Jr. ; produced by Mel Stuart and Richard Schickel. --
> [Paramus, N.J.] : Time-Life Films, 1976.
>> 1 videocassette (39 min.) : sd., col. with b&w sequences ; 3/4
> in. -- (Life goes to the movies ; pt. 5)
>
>> Title on container: Movies today.
>> Narrators: Henry Fonda, Shirley MacLaine, Liza Minnelli.
>> Summary: Discusses the life and career of Marilyn Monroe as
> presented in film and in Life magazine as the epitome of the hopes
> and aspirations of her time. Examines various films whose stark
> language, sexuality, and violence reflected the tensions and
> controversies of the 1960s.
>
>> 1. Monroe, Marilyn, 1926-1962. 2. Motion pictures--United
> States--History. I. Haley, Jack. II. Stuart, Mel. III.
> Schickel, Richard. IV. 20th Century-Fox Television. V. Time-Life
> Television. VI. Time-Life Films. VII. Life (Chicago, Ill. :
> 1936) VIII. Title: Movies today. IX. Series.
>
> PN1993.5.U6
> 791.43

Rule numbers for notes: 7.7B4, 7.7B6a, 7.7B17.
  "New" is capitalized in the title proper, because it is the first word in the title main entry, following an initial article. (*AACR 2*, rule A.4D)

Example 29B

```
Type: g      Bib lvl: m Source: d    Lang: eng
Type mat: v  Enc lvl: I Govt pub:    Ctry: xxu
Int lvl: g   Mod rec:   Tech: l      Leng: 039
Accomp:      MEBE: 0    Dat tp: s    Dates: 1976,
Desc: a
  1   010
  2   040      XXX ǂc XXX
  3   007      v ǂb f ǂd c ǂe c ǂf a ǂg h ǂh r ǂi m
  4   043      n-us—
  5   045      x5x6
  6   090      PN1993.5.U6
  7   092      791.43 ǂ2 20
  8   049      XXXX
  9   245 04   The New morality ǂh videorecording / ǂc a presentation of
20th Century-Fox Television and Time-Life Television ; executive pro-
ducer, Jack Haley, Jr. ; produced by Mel Stuart and Richard Schickel.
 10   260      [Paramus, N.J.] : ǂb Time-Life Films, ǂc 1976.
 11   300      1 videocassette (39 min.) : ǂb sd., col. with b&w sequences
; ǂc 3/4 in.
 12   440  0   Life goes to the movies ; ǂv pt. 5
 13   500      Title on container: Movies today.
 14   511 0    Narrators: Henry Fonda, Shirley MacLaine, Liza Minnelli.
 15   520      Discusses the life and career of Marilyn Monroe as pre-
sented in film and in Life magazine as the epitome of the hopes and
aspirations of her time. Examines various films whose stark language,
sexuality, and violence reflected the tensions and controversies of the
1960s.
 16   600 11   Monroe, Marilyn, ǂd 1926-1962.
 17   650  0   Motion pictures ǂz United States ǂx History.
 18   700 11   Haley, Jack.
 19   700 11   Stuart, Mel.
 20   700 11   Schickel, Richard.
 21   710 21   20th Century-Fox Television.
 22   710 21   Time-Life Television.
 23   710 21   Time-Life Films.
 24   730 01   Life (Chicago, Ill. : 1936)
 25   740 01   Movies today.
```

116

Example 30A

Title screens

COPYRIGHT 1969 AMERICAN NATIONAL RED CROSS

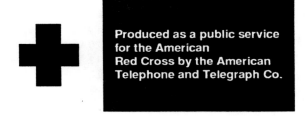

```
Standard first aid multimedia course [motion picture] / produced as a
   public service for the American Red Cross by the American Tele-
   phone and Telegraph Co. -- [Washington, D.C.] : American National
   Red Cross, c1969.
      7 film reels (95 min.) : sd., col. ; 16 mm. + 1 workbook + 1
   first aid textbook + 1 set of materials.

      Summary: Discusses bleeding and shock, conditions that result
   in a need for artificial respiration, poisoning, burns and heat
   exhaustion, situations needing splints, and how to move the in-
   jured.

      1. First aid in illness and injury.  2. Wounds and injuries.
   3. Shock.  4. Life-saving.  5. Artificial respiration.  6. Poison-
   ing.  7. Burns and scalds.  7. Fractures.  8. Splints (Surgery)
   9. Transport of sick and wounded.  I. American Red Cross.  II.
   American Telephone and Telegraph Company.

   RC87
   362.18
```

Example 30A

```
Type: g      Bib lvl: m Source: d    Lang: eng
Type mat: m Enc lvl: I Govt pub:    Ctry: xxu
Int lvl: e  Mod rec:   Tech: l      Leng: 095
Accomp:     MEBE: 0     Dat tp: s    Dates: 1969,
Desc: a
 1   010
 2   040      XXX +c XXX
 3   007      m +b r +d c +e a +f a +g a +h d +i m
 4   090      RC87
 5   092      362.18 +2 20
 6   049      XXXX
 7   245 00   Standard first aid multimedia course +h motion picture / +c
produced as a public service for the American Red Cross by the American
Telephone and Telegraph Co.
 8   260      [Washington, D.C.] : +b American National Red Cross, +c
c1969.
 9   300      7 film reels (95 min.) : +b sd., col. ; +c 16 mm. + +e 1
workbook + 1 first aid textbook + 1 set of materials.
10   520      Discusses bleeding and shock, conditions that result in a
need for artificial respiration, poisoning, burns and heat exhaustion,
situations needing splints, and how to move the injured.
11   650  0   First aid in illness and injury.
12   650  0   Wounds and injuries.
13   650  0   Shock.
14   650  0   Life-saving.
15   650  0   Artificial respiration.
16   650  0   Poisoning.
17   650  0   Burns and scalds.
18.  650  0   Fractures.
19.  650  0   Splints (Surgery)
20.  650  0   Transport of sick and wounded.
21   710 21   American Red Cross.
22   710 21   American Telephone and Telegraph Company.
```

According to the authority file, the heading for the Red Cross changed from "American National Red Cross" to "American Red Cross" about 1984.

Example 30B

Title screens

THE AMERICAN RED CROSS presents

STANDARD FIRST AID
MULTIMEDIA COURSE

Revised 1978

Produced as a public service for
American Telephone and Telegraph Co.

This pair of examples represents two editions of a set of educational films, both with accompanying materials. Uniform title main entries would be needed if an added entry for either had to be made.

Note that, at the end of the statement of responsibility in the first example, and at the end of the edition statement in the second example, one period serves both as the punctuation for the abbreviation **and** the beginning punctuation for the separation between areas. Double punctuation is **not** used in either case.

Rule numbers for notes in the first example: 7.7B17.

Rule numbers for notes in the second example: 7.7B6b, 7.7B17.

The summary for the first example lists many conditions needing first aid. These conditions are all reflected in subject headings. The summary for the second example is more general, and leads to only one subject heading. Each cataloger needs to know the collection and the needs of the users of that collection to judge how extensive a summary is needed and how many subject headings to use to provide appropriate access.

Example 30B

```
Standard first aid multimedia course [motion picture]. -- Rev. --
   [Washington, D.C.] : American Red Cross, 1978.
      3 film reels (60 min.) : sd., col. ; 16 mm. + 1 workbook + 1
   first aid textbook + 1 set of instructor's materials.

      "Produced as a public service for American Telephone and Tele-
   graph Co."
      Summary: Introduces major first aid problems using filmed
   scenes of accidents to demonstrate first aid skills.

      1. First aid in illness and injury.  I. American Red Cross.
   II. American Telephone and Telegraph Company

   RC87
   362.18
```

```
Type: g      Bib lvl: m Source: d    Lang: eng
Type mat: m Enc lvl: I Govt pub:     Ctry: xxu
Int lvl: e  Mod rec:   Tech: l       Leng: 060
Accomp:     MEBE: 0    Dat tp: s     Dates: 1978,
Desc: a
  1    010
  2    040       XXX ǂc XXX
  3    007       m ǂb r ǂd c ǂe a ǂf a ǂg a ǂh d ǂi m
  4    090       RC87
  5    092       362.18 ǂ2 20
  6    049       XXXX
  7    245 00    Standard first aid multimedia course ǂh motion picture
  8    250       Rev.
  9    260       [Washington, D.C.] : ǂb American Red Cross, ǂc 1978.
 10    300       3 film reels (60 min.) : ǂb sd., col. ; ǂc 16 mm. + ǂe 1
workbook + 1 first aid textbook + 1 set of instructor's materials.
 11    500       "Produced as a public service for American Telephone and
Telegraph Co."
 12    520       Introduces major first aid problems using filmed scenes of
accidents to demonstrate first aid skills.
 13    650  0  First aid in illness and injury.
 14    710 21  American Red Cross.
 15    710 21  American Telephone and Telegraph Company.
```

Example 31

Label on cassette

```
┌─────────────────────────────┐
│      AMOS N' ANDY           │
│     RASSLIN MATCH          │
│    AND LION TAMER          │
│                             │
│         MEAL                │
│        TICKET               │
└─────────────────────────────┘
```

```
Meal ticket [videorecording] / directed by Charles Barton. — on 1
   videocassette (28 min.) : sd., b&w ; 1/2 in.

     In Amos n' [sic] Andy. -- [United States? : s.n., 198-?].
     Cast: Spence Williams, Jr. (Andy), Tim Moore (Kingfish).
     Credits: Script, Bob Ross, Dave Schwartz ; photographer, Robert
   de Grasse ; editor, Daniel A. Nathen.
     Originally broadcast ca. 1952 on: The Amos 'n Andy show.
     VHS.
     Summary: Kingfish sells five bachelors supper "meal tickets"
   without telling Sapphire.
     Followed by commercials for Blatz Brewing Company and Schenley
   Industries, Inc.

     1. Comedy films.  I. Barton, Charles, 1902-1981.  II. Williams,
   Spence.  III. Moore, Tim.  IV. Amos 'n Andy show (Television
   program)

PN1995.9.C55
791.43617
```

This is an example of one selection from a videorecording done as an "In" analytic. Depending on the needs of the users of a collection, one might want to make added entries for the firms represented by the commercials. Rule numbers for notes: 7.7B6a, 7.7B6b, 7.7B7, 7.7B10f, 7.7B18.

Example 31

```
Type: g      Bib lvl: m Source: d   Lang: eng
Type mat: v Enc lvl: I Govt pub:   Ctry: xxu
Int lvl: g  Mod rec:   Tech: l     Leng: 028
Accomp:     MEBE: 0    Dat tp: s   Dates: 1978,
Desc: a
 1   010
 2   040      XXX   ‡c XXX
 3   007      v ‡b f ‡d b ‡e b ‡f a ‡g h ‡h o ‡i m
 4   090      PN1995.9.C55
 5   092      791.43617 ‡2 20
 6   049      XXXX
 7   245 00   Meal ticket ‡h videorecording / ‡c directed by Charles
Barton.
 8   300      on 1 videocassette (28 min.) : ‡b sd., b&w ; ‡c 1/2 in.
 9   511 1    Spence Williams, Jr. (Andy), Tim Moore (Kingfish).
10   508      Script, Bob Ross, Dave Schwartz ; photographer, Robert de
Grasse ; editor, Daniel A. Nathen.
11   500      Originally broadcast ca. 1952 on: The Amos 'n Andy show.
12   538      VHS.
13   520      Kingfish sells five bachelors supper "meal tickets" without
telling Sapphire.
14   500      Followed by commercials for Blatz Brewing Company and
Schenley Industries, Inc.
15   650  0   Comedy films.
16   700 11   Barton, Charles, ‡d 1902-1981.
17   700 11   Williams, Spence.
18   700 11   Moore, Tim.
19   730 01   Amos 'n Andy show (Television program)
20   773 0    ‡7 nngm ‡a Amos n' [sic] Andy. ‡d [United States? : s.n.,
198-?]. ‡w (OCoLC)nnnnnnn
```

Example 32

Title screens

A Macmillan Films Inc.
Film Study Extract

————————

Spellbound
(United States, 1956)
The Razor Sequence
Copyright 1975, Macmillan Films Inc.

————————

Director: Alfred Hitchcock
Screenplay: Ben Hecht
Photography: George Barnes
Music: Miklos Rozsa
Editor: Hal C. Kern

————————

Distributed by
Macmillan Films Inc.

Container Label

MACMILLAN FILMS, INC.

34 MacQuesten Parkway South
Mount Vernon, New York 10550

SPELLBOUND — EXTRACTS
————————————
TITLE

PR35/024380
————————————
PRINT NO.

Example 32

```
Spellbound [motion picture] : United States, 1956 : the razor se-
    quence / producer, David O. Selznick ; director, Alfred Hitchcock.
    -- [Mount Vernon, N.Y.] : Macmillan Films, c1975.
        1 film reel (10 min.) : sd., b&w ; 16 mm. + 1 study guide.

    "A Macmillan Films Inc. film study extract."
    Title on container: Spellbound--extracts.
    Cast: Ingrid Bergman, Gregory Peck, Michael Chekov.
    Credits: Screenplay, Ben Hecht ; photography, George Barnes ;
music, Miklos Rozsa ; editor, Hal C. Kern.
    Extract from 1945 motion picture produced by United Artists.
    Summary: An amnesia victim (Peck) assumes the identity of a
noted psychiatrist and is accused of the murder of the man he
professes to be. Another psychiatrist (Bergman) attempts to re-
store Peck's memory and uncover some lead that would prove his
innocence. In this extract, the fugitive couple pretend they are
on their honeymoon and seek refuge at the home of Bergman's former
professor.

    1. Horror films.  2. Cinematography--Study and teaching.  I.
Selznick, David O., 1902-1965.  II. Hitchcock, Alfred, 1899-1980.
III. Bergman, Ingrid, 1915-1982.  IV. Peck, Gregory, 1916-  V.
Chekov, Michael, 1891-1955.  V. Hecht, Ben.  VI. Macmillan Films.
VII. United Artists.  VIII. Spellbound (Motion picture).  Selec-
tions.  1975.

PN1995.9.F4
791.43616
```

This is an extract of a film prepared for use in film study classes.
Rule numbers for notes: 7.7B1, 7.7B4, 7.7B6a, 7.7B6b, 7.7B7, 7.7B17.

Example 32

```
Type: g       Bib lvl: m Source: d    Lang: eng
Type mat: I Enc lvl: I Govt pub:    Ctry: xxu
Int lvl: e  Mod rec:   Tech: l     Leng: 010
Accomp:       MEBE: 0     Dat tp: s   Dates: 1975,
Desc: a
 1   010
 2   040      XXX ǂc XXX
 3   007      m ǂb r ǂd b ǂe a ǂf a ǂg a ǂh d ǂi u
 4   090      PN1995.9.F4
 5   092      791.43616 ǂ2 20
 6   049      XXXX
 7   245 00 Spellbound ǂh motion picture : ǂb United States, 1956 : the
razor sequence / ǂc producer, David O. Selznick ; director, Alfred
Hitchcock.
 8   260      [Mount Vernon, N.Y.] : ǂb Macmillan Films, ǂc c1975.
 9   300      1 film reel (10 min.) : ǂb sd., b&w ; ǂc 16 mm. + ǂe 1
study guide.
10   500      "A Macmillan Films Inc. film study extract."
11   500      Title on container: Spellbound--extracts.
12   511 1  Ingrid Bergman, Gregory Peck, Michael Chekov.
13   508      Screenplay, Ben Hecht ; photography, George Barnes ; music,
Miklos Rozsa ; editor, Hal C. Kern.
14   500      Extract from 1945 motion picture produced by United Art-
ists.
15   520      An amnesia victim (Peck) assumes the identity of a noted
psychiatrist and is accused of the murder of the man he professes to be.
Another psychiatrist (Bergman) attempts to restore Peck's memory and
uncover some lead that would prove his innocence. In this extract, the
fugitive couple pretend they are on their honeymoon and seek refuge at
the home of Bergman's former professor.
16   650  0 Horror films.
17   650  0 Cinematography ǂx Study and teaching.
18   700 11 Selznick, David O., ǂd 1902-1965.
19   700 11 Hitchcock, Alfred, ǂd 1899-1980.
20   700 11 Bergman, Ingrid, ǂd 1915-1982.
21   700 11 Peck, Gregory, ǂd 1916-
22   700 11 Chekov, Michael, ǂd 1891-1955.
23   700 11 Hecht, Ben
24   710 21 Macmillan Films.
25   710 21 United Artists.
26   730 01 Spellbound (Motion picture). ǂk Selections. ǂf 1975.
```

Example 33

Title and credits frames

**AGAINST
ALL ODDS**
Inside Statistics

*Program 9:
Correlation*

Written, Produced, and Directed
by
Jill Singer

Produced in Association With
The American Statistical Association
and the
American Society for Quality Control

A Project of
COMAP
Consortium for Mathematics and Its Applications

A Production of
The Chedd-Angier
Production Company
c1988

126

Example 33

Back of container

AGAINST ALL ODDS:
Inside Statistics

Unlock the mysteries of statistics with this public television series on the real-world applications and timeless equations of this essential subject. Highly engaging, the 26 half-hour programs feature mathematical formulas and living examples that motivate mathematics learning. Hosted by Dr. Teresa Amabile of Brandeis University, the programs present the why as well as the how of statistics using computer animation, colorful on-screen computations, and documentary segments. Produced by the Consortium for Mathematics and Its Applications (COMAP) and Chedd/Angier, in cooperation with the American Statistical Association and the American Society for Quality Control. Released: Fall 1989.

© 1989
ISBN 1-55946-096-2
9: Library of Congress 89-700072
10: Library of Congress 89-700073

Program 9: Correlation
Find out how to derive the correlation coefficient and how to interpret it, using the relationship between a baseball player's salary and his home-run statistics as one example. A study of identical twins further illustrates correlation concepts.
Running Time: 28:52

Program 10: Multidimensional Data Analysis
This program recaps the presentation of data analysis by showing the use of computing technology and a case study at Bell Communications Research. A study on environmental stresses in the Chesapeake Bay demonstrates the value of statistical principles.
Running Time: 28:46

To order or to learn ways to use the series as a course for college credit, call 1-800-LEARNER.
Outside the U.S., call 1-805-968-2291.

The Annenberg/CPB Collection

Distributor: Intellimation
P.O. Box 1922
Santa Barbara, CA 93116-1922

This cassette may be played in the U.S. for private or public performance on VCRs and over college, library, and school closed circuit, and ITFS systems without further permission. For information about cable rights, call 1-800-LEARNER. Use of this series as a telecourse requires an additional telecourse license.

9
10

Example 33A

```
Correlation [videorecording] / written, produced, and directed by
    Jill Singer ; a production of the Chedd-Angier Production Company
    -- [Santa Barbara, CA : Intellimation, 1989], c1988.
    on 1 videocassette (28 min., 52 sec.) : sd., col. ; 1/2 in. --
(Against all odds ; program 9)

        Closed-captioned for the hearing impaired.
        "Produced in association with the American Statistical Associa-
    tion and the American Society for Quality Control. A project of
    COMAP, the Consortium for Mathematics and Its Applications."
        At head of title: The Annenberg/CPB Project.
        Host: Teresa M. Amabile.
        Originally produced for public television.
        VHS.
        Summary: Shows how to derive the correlation coefficient and
    how to interpret it using, as one example, the relationship be-
    tween a baseball player's salary and his home-run statistics. Also
    looks at studies of identical twins for further illustrations of
    correlation concepts.
        With: Multidimensional data analysis.

        1. Correlation (Statistics)  2. Regression analysis.  3. Video
    recordings for the hearing impaired.  I. Singer, Jill.  II
    Amabile, Teresa M.  III. Chedd-Angier Production Company.  IV.
    Intellimation.  V. American Statistical Association.  VI. American
    Society for Quality Control.  VII. Consortium for Mathematics and
    Its Applications (U. S.)  VIII. Annenberg/CPB Project.  IX. Se-
    ries.

QA276
519.537
```

This example shows cataloging of one part of a videocassete, using the "with" note. This is one of 26 programs packaged in 13 videocassettes. The set can be cataloged on one bibliographic record, with a contents note listing the 26 titles, each program can be cataloged separately as shown above, or each cassette can be cataloged as shown in Example 33B.

Order of notes in this example: 7.7B2, 7.7B6, 7.7B6, 7.7B6, 7.7B10f, 7.7B17, 7.7B21.

Example 33A

```
Type: g       Bib lvl: m Source: d    Lang: eng
Type mat: v   Enc lvl: I Govt pub:    Ctry: cau
Int lvl: f    Mod rec:   Tech: c      Leng: 029
Accomp:       MEBE: 0    Dat tp: p    Dates: 1989,1988
Desc: a
 1    010      89-700072
 2    040      XXX ǂc XXX
 3    007      v ǂb f ǂd c ǂe b ǂf a ǂg h ǂh o ǂi u
 4    090      QA276
 5    092      519.537 ǂ2 20
 6    049      XXXX
 7    245 00   Correlation ǂh videorecording / ǂc written, produced, and
directed by Jill Singer ; a production of the Chedd-Angier Production
Company.
 8    260      [Santa Barbara, CA : ǂb Intellimation, ǂc 1989], c1988.
 9    300      on 1 videocassette (28 min., 52 sec.) : ǂb sd., col. ; ǂc
1/2 in.
10    440  0   Against all odds ; ǂv program 9
11    500      Closed-captioned for the hearing impaired.
12    500      "Produced in association with the American Statistical
Association and the American Society for Quality Control. A project of
COMAP, the Consortium for Mathematics and Its Applications."
13    500      At head of title: The Annenberg/CPB Project.
14    511 0    Host: Teresa M. Amabile.
15    500      Originally produced for public television.
16    538      VHS.
17    520      Shows how to derive the correlation coefficient and how to
interpret it using, as one example, the relationship between a baseball
player's salary and his home-run statistics. Also looks at studies of
identical twins for further illustrations of correlation concepts.
18    501      With: Multidimensional data analysis.
19    650  0   Correlation (Statistics).
20    650  0   Regression analysis.
21    650  0   Video recordings for the hearing impaired.
22    700 11   Singer, Jill.
23    700 11   Amabile, Teresa M.
24    710 21   Chedd-Angier Production Company.
25    710 21   Intellimation.
26    710 21   American Statistical Association.
27    710 21   American Society for Quality Control.
28    710 21   Consortium for Mathematics and Its Applications (U. S.)
29    710 21   Annenberg/CPB Project.
```

Example 33B

Correlation ; Multidimensional data analysis [videorecording] /
    written, produced, and directed by Jill Singer ; a production of
    the Chedd-Angier Production Company. -- [Santa Barbara, CA :
    Intellimation, 1989], c1988.
        1 videocassette : sd., col. ; 1/2 in. -- (Against all odds ;
    program 9-10)

        Closed-captioned for the hearing impaired.
        "Produced in association with the American Statistical Associa-
    tion and the American Society for Quality Control. A project of
    COMAP, the Consortium for Mathematics and Its Applications."
        At head of title: The Annenberg/CPB Project.
        Host: Teresa M. Amabile.
        Originally produced for public television.
        VHS.
        Summary: The first program shows how to derive the correlation
    coefficient and how to interpret it, using examples from baseball
    and from a Minnesota study of identical twins (28 min., 52 sec.).
    The second program shows a case study at Bell Communications
    Research and a study on environmental stresses in Chesapeake Bay
    to demonstrate the value of statistical principles (28 min., 46
    sec.).

        1. Mathematical statistics. 2. Correlation (Statistics) 3.
    Regression analysis. 4. Video recordings for the hearing im-
    paired. I. Singer, Jill. II Amabile, Teresa M. III. Chedd-
    Angier Production Company. IV. Intellimation. V. American Sta-
    tistical Association. VI. American Society for Quality Control.
    VII. Consortium for Mathematics and Its Applications (U. S.)
    VIII. Annenberg/CPB Project. IX. Correlation. 1989. X. Multidi-
    mensional data analysis. 1989. XI. Series.

QA276
519.537

Order of notes: 7.7B2, 7.7B6, 7.7B6, 7.7B6, 7.7B7, 7.7B10f, 7.7B17.

Example 33B

```
Type: g       Bib lvl: m  Source: d    Lang: eng
Type mat: v  Enc lvl: I  Govt pub:    Ctry: cau
Int lvl: f   Mod rec:    Tech: c      Leng: 058
Accomp:      MEBE: 0     Dat tp: p    Dates: 1989,1988
Desc: a
```

```
 1    010      89-700072 ‡a 89-700073
 2    040      XXX ‡c XXX
 3    007      v ‡b f ‡d c ‡e b ‡f a ‡g h ‡h o ‡i u
 4    090      QA276
 5    092      519.537 ‡2 20
 6    049      XXXX
 7    245 00   Correlation ; Multidimensional data analysis ‡h
videorecording / ‡c written, produced, and directed by Jill Singer ; a
production of the Chedd-Angier Production Company.
 8    260      [Santa Barbara, CA : ‡b Intellimation, ‡c 1989], c1988.
 9    300      1 videocassette : ‡b sd., col. ; ‡c 1/2 in.
10    440 0    Against all odds ; ‡v program 9-10
11    500      Closed-captioned for the hearing impaired.
12    500      "Produced in association with the American Statistical
Association and the American Society for Quality Control. A project of
COMAP, the Consortium for Mathematics and Its Applications."
13    500      At head of title: The Annenberg/CPB Project.
14    511 0    Host: Teresa M. Amabile.
15    500      Originally produced for public television.
16    538      VHS.
17    520      The first program shows how to derive the correlation coef-
ficient and how to interpret it, using examples from baseball and from a
Minnesota study of identical twins (28 min., 52 sec.). The second pro-
gram shows a case study at Bell Communications Research and a study on
environmental stresses in Chesapeake Bay to demonstrate the value of
statistical principles (28 min., 46 sec.).
18    650 0    Mathematical statistics.
19    650 0    Correlation (Statistics).
20    650 0    Regression analysis.
21    650 0    Video recordings for the hearing impaired.
22    700 11   Singer, Jill.
23    700 11   Amabile, Teresa M.
24    710 21   Chedd-Angier Production Company.
25    710 21   Intellimation.
26    710 21   American Statistical Association.
27    710 21   American Society for Quality Control.
28    710 21   Consortium for Mathematics and Its Applications (U. S.)
29    710 21   Annenberg/CPB Project.
30    730 01   Correlation. ‡f 1989.
31    730 01   Multidimensional data analysis. ‡f 1989.
```

Example 34

Title screens

OCLC Report

An OCLC Video Communications Program
1986 November

Example 34A
Cataloged as a serial

```
OCLC report [videorecording]. -- No. 1 (1986 Nov.)-      . -- Dublin,
   Ohio : OCLC, 1986-
         videocassettes : sd., col. ; 1/2 in.

      Irregular.
      "An OCLC video communications program."
      VHS.

      1. OCLC--Periodicals.  2. Libraries--Automation--Periodicals.
   I. OCLC.

Z699.4.O3
025.3
```

Rule numbers for notes: 12.7B1, 7.7B1, 7.7B10f.

```
Type: a   Bib lvl: s Source: d   Lang: eng
Repr:     Enc lvl:   Govt pub:   Ctry: ohu
Indx: u   Mod rec:   Conf pub: 0 Cont:
ISDS:     Cum ind: u Titl pag: u Phys med:
Ser tp: p Alphabt:   Frequn:     Regulr: x
Desc: a   S/L ent: 0 Pub st: c   Dates: 1986-9999
   1   040     XXX ‡c XXX
   2   090     Z699.4.O3
   3   092     025.3 ‡2 20
   4   049     XXXX
   5   245 00  OCLC report ‡h videorecording.
   6   260 00  Dublin, Ohio : ‡b OCLC, ‡c 1986-
   7   300        videocassettes : ‡b sd., col. ; ‡c 1/2 in.
   8   310     Irregular.
   9   362 0   No. 1 (1986 Nov.)-
  10   500     "An OCLC video communications program."
  11   500     VHS.
  12   610 20  OCLC ‡x Periodicals.
  13   650  0  Libraries ‡x Automation ‡x Periodicals.
  14   710 20  OCLC.
```

The VHS note must be coded 500 in serials format. Format integration will allow us to use 538 in all cases.

Example 34B
Cataloged as a monograph

```
OCLC report. No. 1 [videorecording]. -- Dublin, Ohio : OCLC, 1986.
     1 videocassette (20 min.) : sd., col. ; 1/2 in.

     "An OCLC video communications program."
     Host: Deb Bohli.
     "1986 November."
     VHS.
     Summary: The first issue of a video news magazine features a
tour of OCLC's card production facilities, a visit to the library
of the American Museum of Natural History, reports on the fall
OCLC Users Council meeting, and on the conference Information
Resources for the Campus of the Future.
     On label: OCLC #41699280 [i.e., 14699280].

     1. OCLC.  2. Catalog cards--Reproduction.  3. American Museum
of Natural History.  Library.  4. OCLC.  Users Council.  5. Infor-
mation Resources for the Campus of the Future (1986 : Racine,
Wis.)   I. Bohli, Deb.  II. OCLC.

Z674.82
021.6
```

Rule numbers for notes: 7.7B6a, 7.7B9, 7.7B10f, 7.7B17, 7.7B19.

Example 34B
Cataloged as a monograph

```
Type: g        Bib lvl: m Source: d    Lang: eng
Type mat: v  Enc lvl: I Govt pub:    Ctry: ohu
Int lvl: f    Mod rec:    Tech: l      Leng: 020
Accomp:        MEBE: 0    Dat tp: s  Dates: 1986,
Desc: a
  1   010
  2   040      XXX ‡c XXX
  3   007      v ‡b f ‡d c ‡e b ‡f a ‡g h ‡h o ‡i m
  4   090      Z674.82
  5   092      021.6 ‡2 20
  6   049      XXXX
  7   245 00   OCLC report. ‡n No. 1 ‡h videorecording.
  8   260      Dublin, Ohio :‡b OCLC, ‡c 1986.
  9   300      1 videocassette (20 min.) : ‡b sd., col. ; ‡c 1/2 in.
 10   500      "An OCLC video communications program."
 11   500      Host: Deb Bohli.
 12   500      "1986 November."
 13   538      VHS.
 14   520      The first issue of a video news magazine features a tour of
OCLC's card production facilities, a visit to the library of the Ameri-
can Museum of Natural History, reports on the fall OCLC Users Council
meeting, and on the conference Information Resources for the Campus of
the Future.
 15   500      On label: OCLC #41699280 [i.e., 14699280].
 16   610 20   OCLC.
 17   650  0   Catalog cards ‡x Reproduction.
 18   610 20   American Museum of Natural History. ‡b  Library.
 19   610 20   OCLC. ‡b Users Council.
 20   611 20   Information Resources for the Campus of the Future ‡d (1986
: ‡c Racine, Wis.)
 21   700 11   Bohli, Deb.
 22   710 21   OCLC.
```

Example 35

Title screens

Voices On The River
———
A Film By Gregory Mason
———
Production Assistance
Erik Adolphson
Christine Kittleson
William McGinley
———
Acknowledgements
The Audio Visual Department
and the Biology Department
of Gustavus Adolphus College
KRBI Radio St. Peter Le Sueur
Watercolors by Seth Eastman
Sketches by Frank Mayer
and photographs from
The Minnesota Historical Society
———
Produced under a Grant from
Gustavus Adolphus College
Copyright 1976 Gregory Mason
———
The Minnesota American Revolution
Bicentennial Commission

Example 35

```
Mason, Gregory Henry.
    Voices on the river [motion picture] / a film by Gregory Mason. --
[St. Peter, Minn. : G.H. Mason], c1976.
    1 film reel (22 min.) : sd., col. ; 16 mm.

    Production assistance: Erik Adolphson, Christine Kittleson, Wil-
liam McGinley.
    Filmed with support from Gustavus Adolphus College Research Fund
and the Minnesota American Revolution Bicentennial Commission.
    Summary: Evokes the eventful past of the Minnesota River, from
which the state takes its name. Highlights St. Peter as a typical
river settlement.

    1. Saint Peter (Minn.)--History.  2. Minnesota--History.  3.
Minnesota River Valley--History.  I. Adolphson, Erik.  II. Kittleson,
Christine.  III. McGinley, William A., 1943-  IV. Gustavus Adolphus
College.  Research Fund.  V. Minnesota American Revolution Bicenten-
nial Commission.  VI. Title.

F612.M4
977.63
```

This local production has personal main entry. The production assistants normally would be ignored in cataloging. However, these are local people, and local needs suggest making the note and added entries for them.

Rule numbers for notes: 7.7B6, 7.7B7, 7.7B17.

Example 35

```
Type: g      Bib lvl: m  Source: d    Lang: eng
Type mat: m  Enc lvl: I  Govt pub:    Ctry: mnu
Int lvl: e   Mod rec:    Tech: l      Leng: 022
Accomp:      MEBE: 0     Dat tp: s    Dates: 1976,
Desc: a
  1    010
  2    040       XXX ǂc XXX
  3    007       m ǂb r ǂd c ǂe a ǂf a ǂg a ǂh d ǂi m
  4    043       n-us-mn
  5    090       F612.M4
  6    092       977.63 ǂ2 20
  7    049       XXXX
  8    100 1     Mason, Gregory Henry.
  9    245 10    Voices on the river ǂh motion picture / ǂc a film by Gre-
gory Mason.
 10    260       [St. Peter, Minn. :ǂb G.H. Mason], ǂc c1976.
 11    300       1 film reel (22 min.) : ǂb sd., col. ; ǂc 16 mm.
 12    500       Production assistance: Erik Adolphson, Christine Kittleson,
William McGinley.
 13    500       Filmed with support from Gustavus Adolphus College Research
Fund and the Minnesota American Revolution Bicentennial Commission.
 14    520       Evokes the eventful past of the Minnesota River, from which
the state takes its name. Highlights St. Peter as a typical river
settlement.
 15    651 0     Saint Peter (Minn.) ǂx History.
 16    651 0     Minnesota ǂx History.
 17    651 0     Minnesota River Valley ǂx History.
 18    700 11    Adolphson, Erik.
 19    700 11    Kittleson, Christine.
 20    700 11    McGinley, William A., ǂd 1943-
 21    710 21    Gustavus Adolphus College. ǂb Research Fund.
 22    710 21    Minnesota American Revolution Bicentennial Commission.
```

Example 36

[No title screen]

```
[Butterfield reunion][videorecording]. -- [1988].
    1 videocassette (120 min.) : sd., col. ; 1/2 in.

    Title supplied by cataloger.
    VHS.
    Summary: A reunion of the descendants of George and Ida Countryman
Butterfield to celebrate the 90th birthday of their oldest daughter,
Ruth Manila Butterfield Siemens, on August 6, 1988, at the First
Baptist Church, Lake Crystal, Minn.

    1. Siemens, Ruth Manila Butterfield, 1898-  2. Butterfield family.

CS71.B
929.2
```

This is a typical home video with no title screen. The title must be supplied.
Rule numbers for notes: 7.7B3, 7.7B10f, 7.7B17.

```
Type: g       Bib lvl: m Source: d    Lang: eng
Type mat: v Enc lvl: I Govt pub:      Ctry: xx?
Int lvl: e  Mod rec:   Tech: 1        Leng: 120
Accomp:       MEBE: 0    Dat tp: s    Dates: 1988,
Desc: a
 1   010
 2   040      XXX $c XXX
 3   007      v $b f $d c $e b $f a $g h $h o $i m
 4   090      CS71.B
 5   092      929.2 $2 20
 6   049      XXXX
 7   245 00   [Butterfield reunion] $h videorecording
 8   260      $c [1988].
 9   300      1 videocassette (120 min.) : $b sd., col. ; $c 1/2 in.
10   500      Title supplied by cataloger.
11   538      VHS.
12   520      A reunion of the descendants of George and Ida Countryman
Butterfield to celebrate the 90th birthday of their oldest daughter,
Ruth Manila Butterfield Siemens, on August 6, 1988, at the First Bap-
tist Church, Lake Crystal, Minn.
13   600 10  Siemens, Ruth Manila Butterfield, $d 1898-
14   630 00  Butterfield family.
```

Example 37

Title screens

A Community-Family Farm

———————

Produced & Directed by
Gary J. Way

———————

By
Gary J. Way

———————

in
Partial Fulfillment
of the
Master of Science
Degree...
St. Cloud
State
University

Title page of research report

THE COMMUNITY-FAMILY FARM;
A VIDEO TAPE COMPARISON

A Creative Project
Presented to
the Faculty of the Center for Library
and Audiovisual Education
College of Education
Saint Cloud State University

In Partial Fulfillment
of the Requirements for the Degree
Master of Science

by
Gary J. Way

Center for Library & Audiovisual Education
College of Education
St. Cloud State University
St. Cloud, Minnesota

July, 1977

Example 37

```
Way, Gary J.
    A community-family farm [videorecording] / produced & directed by
Gary J. Way. -- 1977.
    1 videocassette (10 min.) : sd., b&w ; 3/4 in. + 1 research report
(18 leaves ; 28 cm.)


    Title of research report: The community-family farm ; a video tape
comparison.
    Thesis (M.S.)--St. Cloud State University, 1977.
    Summary: A study of the Spengler farm located in North Dakota;
covers the period 1880-1919.
    Research report includes bibliography.


    1. Farm life--North Dakota.  2. Farms--North Dakota.  3. Spengler
family.  I. Title.


S451.N9
631.49
```

Rule numbers for notes: 7.7B11, 7.7B13, 7.7B17, 2.7B18.
This is an example of a video thesis. It is unpublished, so it has no place or name of publisher in area 4.

```
Type: g       Bib lvl: m Source: d    Lang: eng
Type mat: v   Enc lvl: I Govt pub:    Ctry: mnu
Int lvl: e    Mod rec:   Tech: l      Leng: 007
Accomp:       MEBE: 0    Dat tp: s    Dates: 1977
Desc: a
 1    010
 2    040      XXX ǂc XXX
 3    007      v ǂb f ǂd b ǂe c ǂf a ǂg h ǂh r ǂi m
 4    043      n-us-nd
 5    045      w8x1
 6    090      S451.N9
 7    092      631.49 ǂ2 20
 9    049      XXXX
10    100 10   Way, Gary J.
11    245 12   A community-family farm ǂh videorecording / ǂc produced &
directed by Gary J. Way.
12    260      ǂc 1977.
13    300      1 videocassette (10 min.) : ǂb sd., b&w ; ǂc 3/4 in. + ǂe 1
research report (18 leaves ; 28 cm.)
14    500      Title of research report: The community-family farm : a
video tape comparison.
15    502      Thesis (M.S.)--St. Cloud State University, 1977.
16    520      A study of the Spengler farm located in North Dakota; cov-
ers the period 1880-1919.
17    500      Research report includes bibliography.
18    650  0   Farm life ǂz North Dakota.
19    650  0   Farms ǂz North Dakota.
20    600 30   Spengler family.
```

140

Example 38

Title screens

> presented by MTI Teleprograms Inc.
> ─────────
> HANDLING FIREARMS
> ─────────
> script CHARLES REMSBERG
> production mgr. SPEC. AGENT RON ADAMS
> asst. director
> camera
> lighting
> sound
> editor
> special effects SPEC. AGENT RON ADAMS
>
> Additional technical assistance provided by:
> Smith & Wesson ...
> ─────────
> Director Dennis Anderson
> ─────────
> Producer Motorola Teleprograms Inc.

Slide

> HANDLING
> FIREARMS
>
> © MCMLXXIX   MTI Teleprograms Inc.

Guide

HANDLING FIREARMS
**A complete training program consisting of film,
slides, and instructor's manual.**

MTI Teleprograms Inc.

HANDLING FIREARMS

Authors: **Special Agent Ron Adams
Riverside, California Police Department
and
Charles Remsberg**

Example 38

```
Handling firearms [motion picture] / producer, Motorola Teleprograms,
    Inc. ; director, Dennis Anderson ; script, Charles Remsberg. --
    Schiller Park, Ill. : MTI Teleprograms, c1979.
        1 film reel (32 min.) : sd., col. ; 16 mm. + 50 slides (col.) +
    1 guide (52 p. : ill. ; 28 cm.)

        Guide by Ron Adams and Charles Remsberg includes notes on the
    film, script for the slides, and bibliography.
        Summary: Includes how to avoid accidental discharges in a
    variety of situations, safe handling of firearms, firearm storage,
    and serviceability check. Each slide shows a different firearm,
    most of which are street firearms.

        1. Firearms--Safety measures.  I.Anderson, Dennis.  II.
    Remsberg, Charles, 1932-  III. Adams, Ron.  IV. Motorola
    Teleprograms, Inc.  V. MTI Teleprograms.

TS534.5
363.3
```

This example could be cataloged as a kit containing a motion picture, slides, and guide. I considered the motion picture to be the predominant item, so I cataloged the set as a motion picture with accompanying material.

Rule numbers for notes: 7.7B11, 7.7B17.

```
Type: g      Bib lvl: m Source: d    Lang: eng
Type mat: m Enc lvl: I Govt pub:     Ctry: ilu
Int lvl: f  Mod rec:   Tech: l       Leng: 032
Accomp:      MEBE: 0    Dat tp: s     Dates: 1979,
Desc: a
 1   010
 2   040      XXX ‡c XXX
 3   007      m ‡b r ‡d c ‡e a ‡f a ‡g a ‡h d ‡i m
 4   090      TS534.5
 5   092      363.3 ‡2 20
 6   049      XXXX
 7   245 00 Handling firearms ‡h motion picture / ‡c producer, Motorola
Teleprograms, Inc. ; director, Dennis Anderson ; script, Charles
Remsberg.
 8   260      Schiller Park, Ill. : ‡b MTI Teleprograms, ‡c c1979.
 9   300      1 film reel (32 min.) : ‡b sd., col. ; ‡c 16 mm. + ‡e 50
slides (col.) + 1 guide (52 p. : ill. ; 28 cm.)
10   500      Guide by Ron Adams and Charles Remsberg includes notes on
the film, script for the slides, and bibliography.
11   520      Includes how to avoid accidental discharges in a variety of
situations, safe handling of firearms, firearm storage, and serviceabil-
ity check. Each slide shows a different firearm, most of which are
street firearms.
12   650  0 Firearms ‡x Safety measures.
13   700 11 Anderson, Dennis.
14   700 11 Remsberg, Charles, ‡d 1932-
15   700 11 Adams, Ron.
16   710 21 Motorola Teleprograms, Inc.
17   710 21 MTI Teleprograms.
```

Example 39

Information from illustrated script

Effective Visual Presentations	Kodak V1-30
A Visual Communication Program from Kodak	

Cassette tape

```
EFFECTIVE VISUAL PRESENTATIONS
          (10-10)

℗  Eastman Kodak Company 1978
```

Film container

```
Lemon Sequence        V10-10

EFFECTIVE  VISUAL  PRESENTATIONS
```

Back of box cover

MOTION PICTURE AND AUDIOVISUAL MARKETS DIVISION
Rochester, New York 14650

Effective Visual Presentations
Kodak Publication No. V1-30   0544-4-79-F-Major Revision
PRINTED IN U.S.A.

Script verso

© Eastman Kodak Company, 1979

Slide #01

Effective
Visual
Presentations
© Eastman Kodak Company, 1979

Example 39

```
Effective visual presentations [kit] / Eastman Kodak Company, Motion
   Picture and Audiovisual Markets Division. -- Major rev. -- Roches-
   ter, N.Y. : Eastman Kodak, 1979.
      1 motion picture, 133 slides, 1 sound cassette, 1 script ; in
   container 29 x 28 x 8 cm.

      Title on film container: Lemon sequence.
      A sound projector with dissolve control is recommended.
      Summary: Designed to present the basics of planning, producing,
   and presenting visual presentations.

      1. Visual aids.  I. Eastman Kodak Company.  Motion Picture and
   Audiovisual Markets Division.  II. Title: Lemon sequence.

LB1043
371.335
```

This example is of a package of material that includes a motion picture. It is cataloged as a kit because no one component is predominant.

The name of the publisher is given in shortened form in area 4 because it is given in full form in the statement of responsibility.

Rule numbers for notes: 7.7B5, 7.7B10h, 7.7B17.

According to 1.10C2, we can't give complete physical description in area 5. It would be useful if we could use:

```
   1 motion picture (1 film reel (5 min.) : sd., col. ; 16
mm.), 133 col. slides, 1 sound cassette (analog), 1 script (31
p. : ill. ; 28 cm.) ; in container 29 x 28 x 8 cm.
```

Example 39

```
Type: o       Bib lvl: m Source: d    Lang: eng
Type mat: b Enc lvl: I Govt pub:     Ctry: nyu
Int lvl: g  Mod rec:   Tech: n       Leng: ---
Accomp:     MEBE: 0    Dat tp: s     Dates: 1979,
Desc: a
 1    010
 2    040     XXX ǂc XXX
 3    007     m ǂb r ǂd c ǂe a ǂf a ǂg a ǂh d ǂi u
 4    007     s ǂb s ǂd l ǂe m ǂf n ǂg j ǂh l
 5    090     LB1043
 6    092     371.335 ǂ2 20
 7    049     XXXX
 8    245 00  Effective visual presentations ǂh kit / ǂc Eastman Kodak
Company, Motion Picture and Audiovisual Markets Division.
 9    250     Major rev.
10    260     Rochester, N.Y. : ǂb Eastman Kodak, ǂc 1979.
11    300     1 motion picture, 133 slides, 1 sound cassette, 1 script ;
ǂc in container 29 x 28 x 8 cm.
12    500     Title on film container: Lemon sequence.
13    500     A sound projector with dissolve control is recommended.
14    520     Designed to present the basics of planning, producing, and
presenting visual presentations.
15    650  0  Visual aids.
16    710 21  Eastman Kodak Company. ǂb Motion Picture and Audiovisual
Markets Division.
17    740 01  Lemon sequence.
```

Two 007s are used, one for the motion picture and one for the slides with narration on sound cassette.

Example 40

Title screens

Instructional Media Productions
●
Chandler Publishing Company
San Francisco, Calif.
Distributor

TRANSPARENCIES:
SPIRIT DUPLICATOR

Top of cartridge

Technicolor Corp.

Bottom of cartridge

produced by
INSTRUCTIONAL MEDIA
PRODUCTIONS

distributed by
CHANDLER PUBLISHING CO.
124 SPEAR STREET
San Francisco, Calif.
94105

Example 40

```
Transparencies, spirit duplicator [motion picture] / produced by
    Instructional Media Productions. -- San Francisco, Calif. : Chan-
    dler, 1964.
        1 film loop (2 min., 25 sec.) : sd., col. ; 8 mm. + 1 guide. --
    (Audiovisual production techniques)

        Correlated with: Planning and producing audiovisual materials /
    J.E. Kemp.
        A loop film mounted in Technicolor cartridge.
        Summary: Shows how to use a spirit duplicator machine for
    preparing a transparency on frosted acetate from a spirit master
    in three colors.

        1. Transparencies.  2. Fluid copying process.  3. Audio-visual
    education.  I. Kemp, Jerrold E.  Planning and producing audiovi-
    sual materials.  II. Instructional Media Productions.  III. Chan-
    dler.  IV. Series.

LB1044.9.T73
371.335
```

This film loop belongs to an earlier technology, but, because many collections still include film loops, I have included this example.

The punctuation is changed in the title proper to avoid the incorrect use of prescribed punctuation.

The chief source of information for this item includes the container and its labels as integral parts of the motion picture.

Rule numbers for notes: 7.7B7, 7.7B10k, 7.7B17.

Example 40

```
Type: g      Bib lvl: m Source: d     Lang: eng
Type mat: m Enc lvl: I Govt pub:     Ctry: cau
Int lvl: f  Mod rec:   Tech: l       Leng: 003
Accomp:     MEBE: 0    Dat tp: s     Dates: 1964,
Desc: a
 1    010
 2    040      XXX ǂc XXX
 3    007      m ǂb c ǂd c ǂe a ǂh a
 4    090      LB1044.9.T73
 5    092      371.335 ǂ2 20
 6    049      XXXX
 7    245 00   Transparencies, spirit duplicator ǂh motion picture / ǂc
produced by Instructional Media Productions.
 8    260      San Francisco, Calif. : ǂb Chandler, ǂc 1964.
 9    300      1 film loop (2 min., 25 sec.) : ǂb sd., col. ; ǂc 8 mm. +
ǂe 1 guide.
10    440  0   Audiovisual production techniques
11    500      Correlated with: Planning and producing audiovisual materi-
als / J.E. Kemp.
12    500      A loop film mounted in Technicolor cartridge.
13    520      Shows how to use a spirit duplicator machine for preparing
a transparency on frosted acetate from a spirit master in three colors.
14    650  0   Transparencies.
15    650  0   Fluid copying process.
16    650  0   Audio-visual education.
17    700 11   Kemp, Jerrold E. ǂt Planning and producing audiovisual
materials.
18    710 21   Instructional Media Productions.
19    710 21   Chandler.
```

TITLE INDEX

INDEX